MAKING CHOICES THAT HONOR GOD

Are you bound by indecision?
Afraid you're choosing less than the best?

Here's a method of decision making that will help you:

- *Know when to adjust priorities or take on new responsibilities*
- *Put your time, money, and talents to their best uses*
- *Find contentment in your job, relationships, and status*

Pat Springle

MAKING CHOICES
THAT HONOR GOD

MAKING CHOICES THAT HONOR GOD

Pat Springle

LIFEJOURNEY
BOOKS

David C. Cook Publishing Co.
Elgin, Illinois - Weston, Ontario

LifeJourney Books is an imprint of David C. Cook Publishing Co.
David C. Cook Publishing Co., Elgin, Illinois 60120
David C. Cook Publishing Co., Weston, Ontario

Making Choices that Honor God
© 1990 by Patrick Springle

Edited by Edythe Draper
Cover Design by Russ Peterson
Interior Design by Dawn Lauck and April Frost

First printing, 1990
Printed in the United States of America
94 93 92 91 90 5 4 3 2 1

Springle, Patrick
Making Choices That Honor God
ISBN 1-555-13628-1
     1. Christian life—1960 I. Title.
     BV4501.2.S7139 1988
     248.8'42—dc19 88-28827
     CIP

Acknowledgments

I am deeply indebted to many people for their help and encouragement as I worked on this book.

— Thanks to Mitzi Arellano, whose expertise in hieroglyphics enabled her to read my handwriting and type the manuscript.

— Thanks to the folks in the office, Mark Baker, Jay Hamman, Roger Morrison, Candy Steinman, and Teresa Snow, who have encouraged me to work on this book.

— Thanks to my friend, Dan Hayes, for the way he exemplifies what this book is about.

— Thanks to Robert McGee for his encouragement and insights into all kinds of people, including me.

— Thanks to Richard Price, who gave me constructive theological feedback.

— Thanks to Paul Mouw, who believed in this book and made it happen.

— Thanks to Linda Rose, whose continued understanding and encouragement kept me going.

— Thanks to Edythe Draper and Stan Campbell, whose editorial skills sharpened the focus.

— And thanks to my family, Joyce, Catherine, and Taylor, who love me even when I make bad choices.

To Joyce, my favorite radical

Table of Contents

Chapter 1
Choices Make a Difference

Alfred, Donnie, Tom, and I grew up together in Northeast Georgia. We went to school together, played sports together, and attended Boy Scouts together. We even got our Eagle awards at the same time.

One summer the four of us were all home from college and decided to go canoeing. We strapped Donnie's 16-foot Grumman and my fiberglass canoe on our cars and headed for the Georgia-South Carolina line: the Chatooga River. The Chatooga is one of the great white water rivers in the East. As we drove the final few miles down dirt roads between huge white pines, we could hardly wait to hit the water.

Tom shared my canoe. As I put my life jacket on, I offered one to him. He declined, saying, "I won't need that."

We started out, hitting the first set of rapids within fifty yards. Alfred and Donnie cruised right through, but Tom and I had a problem—a big problem. We were using different paddling styles. My style was to go as fast as possible, cutting the paddles in the water to guide the canoe around rocks with splitsecond timing. It was exhilarating! But Tom had a different philosophy.

As we got to the first set of rapids, I was ready to fly, but Tom began paddling _backwards_. He thought it best to ease through the rapids slowly and carefully. It wasn't long before we lost control of the canoe and smashed into a big rock— sideways! Only three minutes on the river, and both of us were soaked, the canoe was capsized, and our paddles and lunches were floating downstream.

I tried to explain why we had lost control and swamped, but Tom still insisted that we try to ease through the rapids. I finally stopped counting the times we capsized when the number reached twenty, but there were considerably more times than that.

Toward the end of the trip we approached a famous section of the river known by some as "The Narrows" and by others as "The Chute." We paddled into a huge pool with big boulders all around us. We could hear the increasing roar of white water, but we couldn't see where the roar came from.

Then, to the right, between two boulders, a steep slope of frothing water went down like a sliding board between two walls of jagged rock. The noise was deafening. The water churned so much that it came over the sides of our canoe. Slowly we sank, though we were moving incredibly fast.

Then we hit a rock and Tom fell out. He slid ahead of the canoe, but held on. I sat in the stern (now almost totally submerged) and tried to keep the canoe going straight. I heard a bump at the bow and saw Tom's hand slide off the gunnel, but we were through the worst of the rapids.

A few seconds later, I was sitting in the canoe in the neck-deep pool at the bottom of the rapids. Only the tips of each end of the canoe were above water. Paddles, shirts, and cushions floated nearby.

"That was wild, wasn't it, Tom? TOM?" With a rush of adrenaline, a million thoughts flashed through my mind. Where was Tom?!

I screamed for Alfred and Donnie who were, I quickly realized, far downstream by now. So I ripped off my life jacket and dove, looking for Tom—or Tom's body. I came up for air and looked frantically for any sign of him.

Another dive. And another. Thirty seconds passed . . . forty-five . . . a minute. It seemed like an eternity and an instant at the same time.

I came up for air again. About thirty feet away at the bottom of The Chute I saw a hand. Tom's strong arms pulled him up on a rock where he sat motionless for a long, long time. I just stared at him.

When his hand had slipped off the side of the canoe as we came down The Chute, the force of the water had wedged him under a ledge and pinned him there. Through sheer strength, Tom had slowly clawed his way upward.

Finally, Tom came down off the rock and said only, "Let's find that other life jacket." We gathered our things, got back in the canoe, and went on.

The incident that day on the Chatooga River is a lot like life. I knew the river was treacherous, so I had a healthy respect for it. In other words, I was scared so I prepared myself! Tom was overconfident. By choosing not to wear a life jacket, he had risked death.

The rapids of life

The choices we make, even the seemingly insignificant daily ones, ultimately determine the course of our lives. These choices take us through calm water and through rapids. And these choices, made either consciously or unconsciously, are based on our answer to the question: *What will provide real meaning and happiness in my life?*

Many people answer that question in terms of success, pleasure, and approval. But such things are no guarantee of meaning and happiness. The story of Randy, a stockbroker in San Francisco, illustrates the drawbacks in that search for a life-style based on success, pleasure, and approval.

Randy is no ordinary stockbroker. He is smart, good looking, and aggressive. Randy has an incredible ability to make money for his clients, his brokerage firm, and himself. By the time he was twenty-eight, he was the top broker in his territory. He bought a fine home in a fashionable part of the city. He and his wife both drove a Mercedes, and they took wonderful vacations and cruises.

But success and fame had a price tag. Randy regularly worked seventy hours a week studying every prospectus, balance sheet, and investment projection he could get his hands on. He called information sources, and then called clients with his recommendations. After the market closed, Randy studied the market results for the day. Somehow he had found time to have three children, but they were still asleep when he left each morning and sometimes asleep when he returned home. His wife, Jan, had become both mother and father to them.

Randy had become a Christian in college, but his faith had taken a backseat to his many successes and few failures. Finally, Randy realized that he was neglecting the ones who meant the most to him: his family and the Lord. He had his cart hitched to the wrong horse, and that horse was at full gallop! It would have been easier if he had based his life on biblical values and priorities from the outset of his career, but he hadn't. It would be much harder to make changes now. His firm and his clients had grown accustomed to his extra hours of research. They expected it. No, they demanded it.

I saw Randy one day not long ago. We talked about the pressures and expectations of his job. He told me, "I can't believe how I've lived the past eight years! How did I fall into that trap? I know the Lord wants me to spend a lot more time with my family, and I'm sure he wants me to minister to people, but there's no time with my job like it is now." Then he said gravely, "I have some hard choices to make."

It's easy to sit back and analyze Randy's predicament, pointing to a few critical decisions that have determined the course of his life. But as Randy talked to me, I realized that my own choices need careful analysis as well.

Why do I do the things I do? What motivates me? How am I answering the questions of what will provide real meaning and happiness?

I thought of the time when Bob remarked to me in my office, "Pat, I don't see how you do all you do. You get more work done than anybody I know."

I recalled another time when Mark asked, "Why do you take on so many projects? You jump on everything that comes along, and then create some of your own, too."

I remembered being on a plane with Eric, busy writing a position paper while he read a magazine and talked to a friend. After a while, he turned to me and exclaimed, "Bro," (Eric calls everybody "Bro"), "do you work all the time? Loosen up!"

A few weeks ago I talked on the phone with Dan, my friend and boss. At the end of a long conversation about everything except the quality of pizza in the Antarctic, Dan said, "Pat, I'm concerned that you may be doing too much. Don't you think you're on overload?"

"No, Dan," I replied, "I really enjoy all this."

"Well, be careful about taking on too much," Dan said in a rather resigned tone.

How did I respond to these friends who, in their gentle way, reproved me for being a workaholic? Did I slow down? Did I even take what they said as a reproof? No! I considered these comments compliments! Why?

The crucial issue: our purpose in life

As I began looking past the surface issues of life, it was as if blinders were taken off my eyes. Reorganizing my schedule might help me get more done, but why did I want to be more effective? For Christ's sake or for my sake? To please Christ or to please other people? The answers to these questions were painfully obvious.

I found that the critical issue was not scheduling, budgeting, or organizing. These are secondary issues. The primary issue was my bedrock purpose in life: *Why am I here? Who or what am I living for?* Unless each of us deals with these questions, we will not make the right choices regardless of how many times we restructure our lives.

Many books are available to help a person bring order to his life. I read one of the most popular ones which contains more than 200 pages of helpful ideas, yet less than one page is devoted to purpose.

If a person's main purpose is his own success, pleasure, and prestige, he can read such a book, apply the principles, redirect his time, relationships, and money, and yet not redefine his purpose one iota. The alterations may help a person become successful, happier, and more pleasing to people, but he becomes hardened in his selfish purpose.

By asking myself the right questions, I finally thought beyond my own selfish purpose and replaced it with a crisp and clear biblical purpose: To honor Christ in everything—no matter what the cost. And with my newfound sense of purpose came a fresh benchmark to help me evaluate each of life's decisions: *How can I please Christ?*

Some of the things I had valued, like recognition and promotions, are insignificant if my purpose is to honor Christ. Other things, such as time with my family and a cutting edge ministry in the lives of others, were critical if I wanted my life to honor Christ. Such things deserve my time and attention.

I needed to make changes in my schedule and budget, changes rooted in my redefined purpose. Confronting selfish motives was not fun, but it is necessary for anyone who truly wants to follow Christ. The Scriptures loudly and clearly proclaim that Christ is worthy of our loyalty and obedience. He deserves to be honored. But many times we can't see this clear choice because of a number of hidden dangers.

Nobody wants to be deceived. Nobody in his right mind wakes up in the morning and says, "I think I'll subject myself to empty lies today." Yet countless people devote their energies to success, pleasure, and approval by others. Such goals promise fulfillment, but they don't deliver. Instead, the results are devastating.

Please don't misunderstand. Nothing is inherently evil with success, pleasure, or approval. God gives us many good things to enjoy, including frequent success in our endeavors. But when we seek these gifts as our first priority, when they are our passions and dreams, then they become our gods—and cruel gods at that. When we cannot tolerate a hint of failure, pain, or neglect, we push harder and worry more in an ultimately hopeless pursuit.

The struggle is real

The struggle against the seductive enticement of success, pleasure, and approval is real, even for those who hold tight to their determination to honor Christ.

Roy and his family own and operate a furniture store. When they moved back to Georgia after living in Texas for a few years, Roy made a commitment to honor Christ as his first priority. He determined to evaluate business decisions, time, money, and relationships by reviewing each item in the light of the single question, "Will this please Christ?"

Even though his convictions were strong and his intentions clear, he recalled, "It's so easy to get sucked into caring

only for me, for my happiness, and what people think of me.
Last year I could feel myself sliding, but I reevaluated what is
really important to me and made some hard choices to follow
Christ no matter what."

Following Christ means more to Roy than listening to a
sermon once a week. He and his wife read the Scriptures and
pray together every day. They look for opportunities to share
their faith. And Roy leads a discipleship group of businessmen
who are genuinely committed to each other. "These things take
time," Roy observes, "but you have to determine what really
matters and put your time there."

A couple of weeks ago, I had lunch with Tim, Mike,
Hank, and Scott. Tim and Mike are in the real estate business.
Hank and Scott work with Christian organizations on college
campuses. Their vocations are very different, but their purposes
are the same: to bring honor to Christ in every way they can.
They would all rather talk about the Lord and what He is doing
in people's lives than anything else.

Tim and Mike use their business as a platform for ministry, while Hank and Scott have their ministry as their vocation.
I was struck by the common purpose of these four men. They
are each very successful at their primary goal—honoring Jesus.

Making the right choice often demands painful self-
probing, hard questions, and redefining life's goals. It is crucial
to renew each day the commitment to follow Christ. And we
must make daily choices in the midst of deceptions—a climate
where success, pleasure, and approval seem to be life goals. We
need to see our choices clearly and evaluate whether they
represent the world's deceptive value system or God's eternal
values.

To help us make these choices, this book will deal with
three areas:

1. What are some of the deceptions to which we are
   exposed in our culture? Unless these deceptions can

be identified accurately, it will be difficult for any of
us to turn from them to the truth.

2. What are the compelling truths of the Scriptures
concerning the treasure we have in Christ?

3. What are some practical suggestions for living a life of
devotion to Christ?

Perhaps it would be wise to insert some perspectives here
about the nature of Christ's call in our lives. Jesus calls all of us
to a radical commitment to Himself and to His purposes. He
said, "Follow Me;" "Count the cost;" "Lay down your life;"
"Deny yourself."

How are we to understand these admonitions? Are they
harsh, condemning, black-and-white commands, or is there a
sense of process?

Christ calls us to a person, a pattern, and a process. We
are called to _a person_, that is, Jesus Himself. Yes, there are goals,
tasks, abstract ideas, and many facets of theology, but our
calling is first and foremost to Jesus Christ as our loving and
powerful Savior and friend.

We are called to _a pattern_ of life which provides a
relational and motivational context for our choices. The
encouragement of the Holy Spirit and the affirmation of fellow
believers give us the comfort, intimacy, and strength we need
to keep walking with the Lord even though we fail so often.
(That's part of what grace is all about, isn't it?)

Healthy relationships play a crucial role in this pattern of
growth and development. The person the Lord uses most in my
own life is my wife, Joyce, but He also uses a longtime friend,
Michael, who seems to show up almost every time I am at a
significant turning point. God uses relationships like these to
help us get His perspective and strength when we need them
most.

And we are called to *a process*. The choice to follow
Christ may occur in an instant, but the process of learning to
know, love, and serve Him is a lifelong experience. Our progress is sometimes fast, but it is often painfully slow. Unrealistic
expectations of complete and rapid change usually lead to
despair and hopelessness.

The demands of lordship and discipleship are high, but
God is patient, kind, and forgiving. He is willing for us to take
things one step at a time, even when we fall as we try to take
many of those steps.

Many issues in this book can seem black and white,
clear, simple, and decisive, but motives are almost always
complex, with shades of gray. Quick and simple answers seldom
work. These issues need to be viewed in light of our calling to a
person, a pattern, and a process. The radical call of biblical
discipleship is challenging, stimulating, and often difficult,
even in the environment of loving relationships. It is almost
impossible without honesty and affirmation.

The people who read this book may have a variety of
motives. Some want to learn how their lives can count for
eternity. Others are confused about their priorities. Some are
looking for the "whys" of life. Some people are compulsively
driven; they are looking for to-do lists, and just want to be told
what decisions to make. A few men may have been given this
book by their wives to get them to shape up! The book was
written for the first three kinds of readers. The others can
probably find something else to do with their time.

At the end of each chapter you will find a few questions.
Take time to answer them. They will help you consider and
apply the perspectives discussed in the chapter.

QUESTIONS

1. List some characteristics of people who pursue success, pleasure, and approval. (Include desires, free time, family life, job, possessions, relationship with God, etc.)

2. List some characteristics of those who truly want to honor Christ.

3. What are the benefits and costs of each characteristic listed in #1 and #2?

4. How can a person tell if he or she is being deceived?

5. Read John 8:44; Ephesians 6:11, 12; and I Peter 5:8, 9. List some of the characteristics of Satan. What should be our attitude toward him?

6. Christ calls us to a person, a pattern, and a process. Describe what each of these means in your life.

Chapter 2
Choosing Your Treasure

As he had done countless times before, Mel Fisher leaned over the side of the salvage boat, watching the bubbles from the scuba tanks and anxiously waiting for news from the divers. For seventeen years, Fisher and his crew had been chasing "The Big A," the *Nuestra Senora de Atocha*.

This was no ordinary Spanish galleon. When the *Atocha* sank in a hurricane off the Florida Keys in 1622, a fabulous treasure went down with her. Worm-eaten documents in the General Archive of the Indies in Seville, Spain, indicated that the *Atocha* was the escort for a fleet of twenty-eight ships. She was carrying huge quantities of gold, silver, jewels, copper, indigo, and tobacco from Hawaii to Spain. In fact, the treasure was so immense that the Spanish crown, which depended heavily on riches gleaned from the New World, was devastated. The ripple effect caused a depression throughout Europe. With a tantalizing story like that to goad his imagination, Fisher persevered through long years of searching.

Many people scoffed at Fisher's attempts to find the
Atocha. After all, many other treasure hunters had looked for
her and had failed. But on July 20, 1975, Fisher's son Dirk
found a bronze cannon that was irrefutably from "the Big A."
Treasure and fame were surely to be found! But instead of joy
and wealth, there was heartache only a week later when Dirk,
his wife Angel, and diver Rick Gage drowned when their
salvage boat capsized. Still, Fisher pressed on.

His crew endured years of searching, countless dives,
repeatedly scouring undersea topographical charts and sonar
readings, raising money to finance the operations, much sweat,
and many dreams. Yet all they found were a few artifacts, coins,
and jewels—just enough to keep their hopes alive. They were
close, always close, but where was the main treasure?

On July 20, 1985, Fisher tried a new salvage technique.
He rigged the engines of the boat so that the force would blow
sand off the sea floor in a portion of the search area. After
waiting to let the water clear, Fisher sent divers down to see
what the operation had uncovered.

All eyes on the salvage boat were fixed on the bubbles
from the scuba tanks. Suddenly, a diver surfaced, yanked the
regulator out of his mouth and yelled, "It's here! We've found
the main pile!"

As he swam to the ocean floor, the diver saw an amazing
spectacle: stacks of gold and silver (7,000 ounces of gold and
1,038 silver bars), glittering untarnished in the salt water.
There was also a dazzling array of gold and silver candelabra,
dishes, bowls, handfuls of jewels, and 530,000 doubloons.

That day, the divers hauled up so much treasure that the
salvage boat almost sank. The entire treasure would take a
seventy-member team some two and a half years to recover. Its
value was estimated at about $400 million.

Because he had sold shares to investors to raise funds for
the search, Fisher's cut was only 5%—about $20 million. Still,

that's not too bad for a man who lived quite modestly on a houseboat with his wife, Dolores. The couple drove an old car because virtually all they had was spent on finding the *Atocha*. Now he intends to display his part of the treasure in a tourist exhibit that will outdo King Tut.

Mel Fisher had a tenacious, single-minded devotion to finding that treasure. He gave up virtually everything to have it: his time, his money, comfort, his reputation, and even his family. But he found it! After seventeen long years of almost total futility, many people said Fisher was a fool. But on July 20, 1985, they called him a genius.

Know value when you see it

Virtually every person values something so much that he is willing to pay a great price for it. Jesus' followers needed to be taught that there is a treasure of such great value that everything a person has should be given to obtain it. So Christ told them two parallel parables to illustrate the point:

The kingdom of heaven is like a treasure hidden in the field, which a man found and hid; and from joy over it he goes and sells all that he has, and buys that field.

Again, the kingdom of heaven is like a merchant seeking fine pearls, and upon finding one pearl of great value, he went and sold all that he had, and bought it (Matthew 13:44-46).

Like Mel Fisher, the man in the first parable found a magnificent treasure, but unlike Fisher, this man wasn't looking for it. Perhaps the treasure had been hidden during one of the many wars that Palestine had endured. Hiding something in a field was much safer than in a house which would probably be ransacked by marauders.

Whatever the man found, he calculated that its value was more than the sum of all he owned. Seemingly without hesitation, he chose to sell his possessions and bought the land so the treasure would be his.

The pearl merchant had seen thousands of pearls, but one stood out from all the others. In that day fine pearls were rare and usually came from distant oyster beds. Merchants traveled treacherous trade routes to acquire them. But even among fine pearls, this one was exceptional. Like the man who found the hidden treasure, the merchant's calculation of the high value of his find was conclusive. He chose to sell all of his possessions to buy the pearl.

Selling all one's possessions is a drastic action, but the greater value of the treasure and the pearl justified such action. The men in the parables may have endured ridicule as they chose to sell all they owned, but their actions were reasonable in light of the worth of the treasure and the pearl. They would have been fools to pass up the once-in-a-lifetime opportunities.

When the men chose to sell all their possessions, did they act sacrificially? No. Even though they gave up a lot, it was not a sacrifice. Their purchases were directed toward acquiring an object of equivalent value. The implications of the parables is that the treasure and the pearl were worth considerably more than what was paid for them. The selling of all their possessions was simply a prudent decision.

So what is the point of these parables? What do the treasure and the pearl symbolize? Clearly, they symbolize Christ Himself. The tenderness of His love and the magnitude of His power are so awesome and wonderful that the only reasonable response is one of abject, reckless abandonment to Him. To value Him less is to be a fool.

The apostle Paul communicated the spirit of this reasonable response to Christ in his letter to the Philippians. He recounted an impressive list of credentials:

I myself might have confidence even in the flesh. If anyone else has a mind to put confidence in the flesh,

I far more: circumcised the eighth day, of the nation
of Israel, of the tribe of Benjamin, a Hebrew of
Hebrews; as to the Law, a Pharisee; as to zeal, a per-
secutor of the church; as to the righteousness which is
in the Law, found blameless (Philippians 3:4-6).

Paul was a young lion, the brightest star in Judaism, yet
he wrote:

Whatever things were gain to me, those things I
have counted as loss for the sake of Christ (Philippians 3:7).

Paul gave up the credentials that every young man in
Palestine aspired to have. He traded the honor that was due a
man who was sure to rise to the pinnacle of his people for a
treasure of greater value:

More than that, I count all things to be loss in view
of the surpassing value of knowing Christ Jesus my
Lord, for whom I have suffered the loss of all things,
and count them but rubbish in order that I may gain
Christ (Philippians 3:8).

Paul considered the value of knowing, loving, and
serving Christ to be greater than the position and prestige of
being number one.

Not many of us value Christ so highly that every other
honor and pursuit in life is rubbish in comparison, but there are
a few examples. One such man was a brilliant young concert
pianist. He was lauded as the next Chopin. When he played,
the music had another dimension of depth and richness. Praise
from fans and critics continued to grow until he unexpectedly
announced that he had chosen to leave the United States to
become a missionary in a remote region of New Guinea. A
missionary? In New Guinea? Leaving behind a most promising
career?

A newspaper account related the story of his choice to
forsake a blossoming career to serve Christ in obscurity over-

seas, and ended with the conclusion: "What a waste!" But to whom was it a waste? Certainly it was not a waste to the talented young man whose love for Christ overshadowed anything worldly success and prestige could offer. To him, it was a reasonable response. He was not deceived by applause and certain fame.

Deceptive influences

A few years ago my wife, Joyce, and I spent a few days in Highlands, North Carolina. Highlands is in a beautiful part of the state, snuggled next to the Georgia line. The Southern Appalachians are spectacular there with several eye-popping waterfalls (one that you can drive behind), granite cliffs, huge white pines, and some of the best hiking and canoeing in the East. Like most places of magnificent scenery, it attracts flocks of tourists. But where tourists go, you will also find people who know tourists will buy absolutely anything—so that's exactly what they sell.

One morning before a hike, Joyce and I stopped by a few shops in town. One shop had a row of beautiful gold watches displayed in the showcase. As I looked more closely, I noticed a contradiction in the labels. The inscription on the watch faces read, "Rolex." The price tags read, "$39.95." I thought, *These ain't Rolexes!*

That conclusion was an easy one. I wish the truth in all situations was as simple to determine. Deception by its very nature is insidious. We don't recognize certain untruths, otherwise we would not be deceived. Deception in our culture comes in many attractive forms, all promising something they cannot deliver. Corporate ladder climbing, vacations to exciting places, nice homes and cars, beauty, and intimate relationships all seem like they will give us the happiness we seek. But no matter how successful, beautiful, or powerful people become, it never seems to be enough.

Some of James Taylor's music expresses the pain and confusion of shattered dreams. When dreams are shattered, we lose our moorings and often drift into drinking, drugs, and sex to deaden the pain. Taylor sings mournfully: "Every now and then the things I lean on lose their meaning and I find myself careening into places where I should not let me go."

A lot of us do the right things for the wrong reasons. We are overly responsible; we are rescuers who try to serve, work, and help others because we are desperately trying to create a sense of worth. We long to be loved and appreciated, so we respond to others' needs in the hope that meeting their needs will win their affection and approval. We compulsively help others. We need to be needed.

This type of driven people are often considered the "most committed people" in the church or group, but their drive is not based on a sense of strength or compassion. Rather, it usually comes from a deep sense of hurt and a desire to soothe that hurt by pleasing others through serving them.

Those of us who are compulsive fixers or servants tend to do a good job of taking care of others, but may be so busy helping others that we neglect our own emotional, spiritual and physical needs. We need to learn that we are responsible for taking care of ourselves (Gal. 6:5). That isn't selfishness; it is stewardship. Only then can we choose to help others because we want to (Gal. 6:2), not because we are driven to help them, to win their approval, or to feel better about ourselves.

We also need to learn that we can't do everything. We should ask, "Lord, what am I responsible for, and what are others responsible for?"

Compulsive, driven people assume that they are responsible for almost everything and everybody. They feel that it is up to them to make others happy, successful, and good. But that is not up to us. Our concern for others is important, but it should have reasonable limits.

Filling the vacuum

God created us with the compelling need to be secure
and significant, but there is a catch: only He can meet that
need. Blaise Pascal, the renowned French philosopher and
physicist, said, "There is a God-shaped vacuum in the heart of
each man which cannot be filled by any created thing, but only
by God, the Creator, made known through Jesus Christ."

The source of most of our problems is that we try to fill
up the God-shaped vacuum with possessions, positions, and
people, but they don't fit. They don't satisfy our need, so we try
harder, looking for other people, things, or experiences to give
the contentment that only God can give.

The painful effects of wrong values are evident. Some
people are perfectionists, but they never feel they have done
enough. They tend to be highly critical of others, but are even
harder on themselves. Perfectionism often leads to the downward spiral of morbid introspection and self-condemnation.

I have a notebook that I use as a combination planner
and portable file cabinet. At the front of that notebook is a
plain, ordinary piece of paper that is miraculously transformed
into an instrument of great power when I write these words on
it: "To Do List."

Every week I make a fresh list of things that need to be
done, and I add to that list as things come up during the week.
Every day I look at the list and determine what needs to be
done that particular day. One of the great joys of my life is
putting little check marks next to items that have been
accomplished.

This list is supposed to be a great help to me, and most of
the time it is. But sometimes the list rules me instead of my
ruling it. That happens when I look at the list and ponder,
"Have I done enough? If I can only get one more thing checked
off today, then I'll be really satisfied." Trying to fill my
"vacuum" with busyness only leads to frustration.

Some people try to put the acceptance of others in the "God-shaped vacuum," and are devastated by the slightest disapproval. They are easily manipulated because they want to please people at any cost.

Since I am a "good Southern boy" with my roots in Georgia, I have learned the Southern social courtesies of saying the right thing at the right time, which makes everybody happy and comfortable. But sometimes I do so at the expense of truth and honesty—not so much as a social courtesy as to win their approval. I may even exaggerate "a little" to impress them just a bit more.

Still other people are so concerned with appearance that much of their time is spent on looking just right. They compare their clothes, hair, complexion, and shape to everybody else's. But such a preoccupation with appearance does little to fill that God-shaped vacuum.

Don't buy the lies

When I was a child, I was rather rotund. I have vivid and painful memories of being in department stores trying to squeeze into pants the saleslady brought me. After a while, she inevitably would utter those heart-wrenching words, "Well, let's see what we have for you in Huskies." With that, I hung my head and walked toward the racks of Huskies like I was taking my last walk on death row. The pants there looked big enough to make a denim circus tent.

The sting of not being asked to pose for the cover of *GQ* is still rekindled from time to time. Not long ago, my daughter Catherine, studying in our living room about fifteen feet away from me, joyfully said, "Daddy, I can see your bald spot all the way from here." I was not nearly as joyful as she was.

The sad truth is that many Christians are believing the lies that success, approval, and beauty will make us happy. We who have been bought by the blood of Christ and reconciled to

God in a relationship of unconditional love and acceptance are too often like the rest of the world. We also treasure the wrong things. Christ alone can meet our deepest needs, and He alone is worthy of our deepest love and obedience. Yet we often continue to pursue things that cannot possibly give lasting fulfillment. We are deceived.

This error is not usually obvious. Our involvement in church, Bible studies, and other forms of Christian service may appear to be from noble motives, but too often we are only using these activities (and using God) to help us be fruitful and productive Christians (so we can accomplish our own purposes of success, status, and approval). God, however, will not be used for our selfish purposes. He desires to be worshiped and obeyed for His own honor and glory. Christ is our treasure, not our pawn.

Most people are consumed with the desire for success and appreciation, and the means to acquire these precious commodities vary widely. We avoid responsibilities that have a significant risk of failure. We naturally gravitate toward those in which success is more assured. We avoid people who make us feel uncomfortable or inferior. And we seek out those people who make us feel good about ourselves.

A few people strive to do their best in every area of life, but most of us concentrate on one or two aspects (business, sports, academics, family, or other relationships) in an insatiable drive for success and recognition.

Lester Korm, founder and chairman of Korm/Ferry International, one of the largest executive search firms in the United States, said of top business executives: "Their absolute, total dedication [is] being the boss, being at the top, and being in control of their lives. I can't stress enough how controlled these people are."

Korm's statement is revealing, indeed! Many executives want to be in control, but they themselves are controlled by their own passion for success and power. That same controlling passion becomes evident in other ways. Think of how angry or dejected some people get when they lose a "friendly" game of golf, tennis, or volleyball. Or consider the demands some people put on family members to act in a way that makes the family look happy and successful. The passion for success and appreciation is powerful, but so is the withdrawal, depression, and anger that can accompany failure and disapproval.

The painful truth is that many Christians have a consuming passion for success and approval that far overshadows their desire to follow Christ. The reasons are varied for why we often pursue what is ultimately empty and neglect what is ultimately fulfilling. They may include poor parental modeling, spiritual conflict, misunderstanding of Scripture, lack of encouragement, peer pressure, and many more.

Pest control

Craig is a friend of mine. Before he became a Christian, practically every waking moment was designed to achieve a prominent position in business so people would give him the acclaim he wanted. He dreamed of being the CEO of a company, with lots of perks and assistants doing whatever he asked them to do. Of course, others would call him for advice or ask him to speak at the Rotary Club.

When Craig accepted Christ, he soon found himself involved in church-related activities. He was very active, and soon he was assuming responsible positions. People wanted his opinions. They asked him to speak. And after eleven years of leadership positions in church and parachurch organizations, Craig came to the startling conclusion that his deepest motives for being a Christian leader were exactly the same as they had been before he became a Christian. He was still striving for success and recognition, only now he was using Christian service to achieve that end. He was trying to use God to help him meet his own self-serving purposes. When he realized that his purpose was selfish, he repented, choosing to honor Christ no matter what anyone else might think of him.

Could this be a major cause of the spiritual impotence we see in Christianity today? Have we redefined our faith so it fits more comfortably into our culture? Instead of turning from a selfish search for success and approval, we have gladly embraced the world's values as our own. But we try to use God's Word, God's people, and God's Spirit to achieve success and popularity.

By exposing deception in our culture, we will be more likely to return to a proper, humble relationship with God. In that relationship, we'll find a deep sense of security and significance, as well as pure motives for Christian service.

Some people are well aware of their propensity to do the right thing for selfish reasons. The mere mention of impure motives elicits a pang of self-awareness. But the insidious nature of deception runs so deep that we may not even be aware that our motivation is selfish and dishonoring to Christ.

A few weeks ago, I saw a commercial on television advertising a pest control company. It showed two happy American families, one on the right half of the split screen and the other on the left. On each side, the camera showed the family sitting on a comfortable sofa. It also showed the flooring and the foundations of the house under them. The voice described the family on the left, whose house had a solid, strong foundation. No problems there.

Then the announcer turned to the family on the right. He lowered his voice a bit and spoke with urgency as he explained that termites were busily munching away on the foundation of the house of this cheerful, unsuspecting family. Little did they know that a disaster was about to happen!

This commercial is an excellent illustration of the insidious nature of selfish motives. Like the two families on the split screen, the lives of two Christians may outwardly appear very similar. Two people may be involved in the same activities, use the same accepted Christian jargon, and wear the same kind of smiles, yet their foundations may be quite different.

One person's life may be founded on the unconditional love and acceptance of God, with a sincere obedience out of gratitude to God and a bedrock of simplicity and purity of devotion to Christ. The other may be going through the same motions, but only as a means to gain status, success, and appreciation. Like a termite infestation, the problem may not become evident for quite a while. But sooner or later the foundation will crack, then splinter, and then the life will crash in a morass of broken dreams, shame, and the pain of broken relationships with people who have been used and manipulated. The crash, though tragic, is a painful opportunity for awareness and repentance.

Sometimes, due to stamina and ability to play the game, a person's "crash" may not be noticeable. Yet their downfall will come in secret with a devastating blow as they stand before Christ to give an account of their lives (II Corinthians 5:10; I Corinthians 3:10-15). At that point, they will be asked (as all Christians will) to give an account of their motives and priorities.

The termite ad says it is foolish not to get an inspection of your foundation. After all, "It's free!" If termites are found, the solution can be applied. Putting off action allows the termites to do more damage and the remedy will be more severe. It is expensive to rebuild a foundation that has for years been eaten away by termites. That fact should be an incentive to have an inspection as soon as possible so corrections will be relatively painless.

The same truths hold for our spiritual problems. We need to clearly see the choices we have each day—to live by the world's deceptive value system or by God's eternal values.

In later chapters we will identify some of the causes and consequences of selfish purposes, but before we get to the problems, we will examine what the Scriptures say about our true, biblical purpose.

QUESTIONS

1. *If you were Mel Fisher, how would you have felt the day you found the treasure after seventeen long years of searching?*

2. *What are some ways you can tell what someone really values?*

3. *What do you really value?*

4. *Read Philippians 3:1-10. What were Paul's credentials? What was of utmost importance to him? What was his estimation of the worth of everything else? What is of utmost importance to you? What is your estimation of the worth of everything else?*

Chapter 3
Choosing Your Purpose

When Joyce and I moved to Austin, Texas, we wanted to join a good church. After a little looking around, we joined Westlake Bible Church. When we had gotten to know the pastor and several board members, I told them I'd be happy to serve in any area where they needed help. After all, I'd been teaching from the Bible for some time and I had several series that would be good for Sunday school classes. Perhaps I could substitute for the pastor on Sunday morning when he was out of town.

A couple of weeks later I got a call from Joe, the chairman of the elders and coordinator of the Sunday school classes. He explained that there was a need in the church that I would be able to help with.

Joe said, "Pat, I understand that you're available to serve in a Sunday school class."

"Yes, I am," I responded with anticipation. (I was primed for the assignment, eager to know which class I'd be teaching.)

"Great, I appreciate your willingness to help us. I'd like you to be in charge of the toddler class this year."

Joe probably thought the phone went dead because he didn't hear anything for a while. What I wanted to say was, "Are you kidding me? You're not going to stick *me* back there with runny noses, messy diapers, and kids who scream and cry for hours! I'm a Bible teacher!"

But I didn't say that. Out of the recesses of my throat came a guttural noise that sounded like, "Yes, I'll be glad to." I was lying.

The next week Joyce and I began our duties. I asked her to help me, and she, in her infinite kindness, agreed. And as it turned out, the job wasn't as bad as I had imagined. It was worse.

Week after week for a year I anticipated the hour in the toddler class like I would anticipate a weekly root canal with no novocaine. You see, I like to be respected. I like people to appreciate me. But those toddlers didn't give me a lot of affirmation. My sense of self-worth and serenity suffered as they wiped their noses on my pants, bashed each other with blocks and screamed in anguish, perpetually knocked over apple juice, and did absolutely nothing I asked them to do. (I frequently spent this time strategizing horrible kinds of revenge for Joe.)

Joyce was a lifesaver. She patiently cleaned up the toddlers and entertained them with songs, marches, books, and games while I stood sulking in the corner and wondered if it was going to be them or me.

Joyce kept reminding me we were in the toddler class to serve the Lord—with gladness no less! But I wanted to teach! After a few thousand years (actually a few months) in the toddler class, I realized that I had not wanted to serve at all. I had just wanted a platform to earn respect through my teaching. My purpose was tainted with a selfish desire for recognition and respect. It was not to honor Christ.

Determining a focal point

The apostle Paul did not mince words when he wrote to the Corinthian Christians about life's purpose:

I am afraid that just as Eve was deceived by the serpent's cunning, your minds may somehow be led astray from your sincere and pure devotion to Christ (II Corinthians 11:3, *NIV*).

Several observations are noteworthy. First, Paul said, "I am afraid." That in itself is a remarkable statement because Paul wasn't afraid of much. He would enter a city to present the Gospel. Then he would be ridiculed, beaten, and thrown out of town—only to get up, walk to the next city and begin again. He boldly proclaimed, "I am ready not only to be bound, but even to die at Jerusalem for the name of the Lord Jesus" (Acts 21:13). So for Paul to tell the Corinthians that he was afraid of something is quite significant. But what did he fear?

He was afraid that the Corinthians would be deceived, "just as Eve was deceived by the serpent's cunning." The King James Version uses the word *craftiness* rather than *cunning*. The sense here is that Satan, the serpent, was underhanded when he lied to Eve, promising her something he couldn't deliver. Satan told her that if she disobeyed the clear directions of God and ate the forbidden fruit, she would not experience the consequence of death. Furthermore, Satan told Eve, "God knows that in the day you eat from it your eyes will be opened, and you will be like God, knowing good and evil" (Genesis 3:5).

Satan's deception was not just that Eve would avoid punishment for sin, but that she would actually be rewarded by becoming like God. The implication is that she would be free from God's control and direction to manage her own life and seek her own honor: the essence of pride.

It sounded good—so good that Eve eagerly pursued the course she thought would provide autonomy. But her misguided hope ended abruptly in the stark reality of God's judgment.

Paul was afraid for the Corinthians because the evil one was still hard at work, promising fulfillment and autonomy to unsuspecting people. Would Paul be even more frightened for us today? Too many of us believe that if we are successful enough, if we have a nice house, beautiful clothes, and fun-loving friends, then we will be worry-free and independent, the masters of our own lives. We would be "like God."

The antithesis of such idolatry is "sincere and pure devotion to Christ." Paul is referring to a single-minded, uncomplicated, heartfelt, consuming passion for Jesus—not Christ's cause, Christ's principles, Christ's work, Christ's ideals, nor Christ's benefits. Paul simply means Christ Himself. The other aspects of Christian faith take on true meaning only if Christ is the focal point. And to the degree that we seek the blessings of God rather than God Himself, our lives will be out of sync with His will and purpose.

Our ultimate purpose

Much could be written about the theology or philosophy of sincere and pure devotion to Christ, but perhaps the best way to communicate it is to get a glimpse of a man who exemplifies such devotion. Frederick W. Faber spoke these poignant words in one of his sermons:

Wherever we turn in the church of God, there is Jesus. He is the beginning, middle, and end of everything to us. . . .There is nothing good, nothing holy, nothing beautiful, nothing joyous which He is not to His servants. No one need be poor, because, if he chooses, he can have Jesus for his own property and possessions. No one need be downcast, for Jesus is the joy of heaven, and it is His joy to enter into sorrowful hearts. We can exaggerate about many things; but we can never exaggerate our obligation to Jesus, or the compassionate abundance of the love of

Jesus to us. All our lives long we might talk of Jesus, and yet we should never come to an end of the sweet things that might be said of Him. Eternity will not be long enough to learn all He is, or to praise Him for all He has done, but then, that matters not; for we shall be always with Him, and we desire nothing more.

Throughout the Scriptures, man is exhorted to glorify God because of His majesty, love, and power. It is our proper response to Him. The Shorter Version of the Westminster Catechism reflects this response, "The chief end of man is to glorify God and enjoy Him forever." But what does it mean to glorify God?

A helpful analogy is that of a solo accompanist. It is the role of the accompanist to bring out the qualities of the soloist, to enhance every note, crescendo, and pause so the audience will focus its attention and appreciation on the soloist. The mark of an accomplished accompanist is that he is scarcely noticed.

This analogy is an accurate reflection of what it means to glorify God. As we praise and worship Him, and as we reflect His loving and powerful character even in the most mundane events in our lives, He receives glory. Conversely, our ability to give Him honor is nullified by our sins. Like an accompanist, we honor God most when we call attention to His qualities without thought of our own reputation.

Our ultimate purpose, then, is to glorify God. The obvious question is: How can we glorify Him? This is a question that needs some serious consideration. As you begin to focus on this important issue, you might want to examine the following chart, which shows how a relationship with Christ is woven together with obedience, service, and other aspects of our lives.

Meditate on the verses. Think through the connection between all the elements of the chart. Make it personal to you.

PURPOSE: GLORIFY GOD

RELATIONSHIP WITH CHRIST
GOALS: To know and love Christ

Matthew 22:36-39
Philippians 3:7-10
Matthew 13:44-46
John 17:3
Psalm 27:4

(Over flow)

Psalm 73:25, 28
John 7:37-39
Jeremiah 9:23, 24

THE LIFE OF CHRIST IN US

- Obedience
- Godly Lifestyle
- Biblical Values
- Structured Ministry
- Spontaneous Ministry

John 14:15, 21
Matthew 16:24-27
Matthew 6:19-21, 33
Matthew 28:18-20
Matthew 25:37-40

Purpose:	To honor Christ
Focus:	On Christ
Question:	How can I please Him?
Results:	Obedience, Godliness, Biblical values, Ministry, Joy, Contentment, Direction

We glorify God chiefly through our relationship with Christ. A deep and intimate relationship with Christ is the fertile soil of spiritual growth. Some people believe growth itself is their purpose in life. But it isn't.

Growth is the result of the relationship; it is not the primary focus. Again, Christ Himself is that primary focus. The goal of our relationship with Christ, like the goal of any relationship, is to know and love Him.

Spiritual growth is the spontaneous result of understanding and experiencing Christ's unconditional love and awesome power. To state that the goal of a person's relationship with Christ is character development or some other benefit is to miss the clear teaching of the Scripture on this subject. Becoming like Christ is, to be sure, a good thing, but it is not our ultimate goal. (A more comprehensive analysis of the goal of becoming like Christ will be discussed later.)

Childlike observations

Jesus often used children to demonstrate purity and simplicity. (See Matthew 18:1-6; 19:13-15; Mark 10:13-16; and Luke 18:15-17.) Children are unencumbered by elaborate goal setting and character development. They thrive on receiving and expressing love, so they are role models for how we should respond to God.

My children have very different ways of expressing affection for Joyce and me. Catherine is six years old. She often goes to her room, sometimes for hours, to draw elaborate pictures for us. She occasionally folds them and wraps them in paper she has colored. Then she stands at the top of the stairs and yells, "Everybody close your eyes!" She comes down and presents her gifts to us with so much joy that she sometimes giggles uncontrollably.

Taylor, almost five years old, is very different. He likes to draw, but he wants one of us right there with him so we can talk about it. He expresses his love verbally or physically (gorilla hugs). Catherine's love is usually expressed in more artistic ways.

Neither of them ever talk about becoming a better son or becoming a better daughter. They simply respond to being loved by expressing their love in return. We discipline them when they need it, but we try to be sure they know we do it because we love them. Their character development and values are molded in this loving environment.

Last spring at a retreat, our friend Jennifer was responsible for a few hours of child care duty before noon. At lunch she told me, "I spent some time with Taylor this morning. Pat, it is amazing! He talks just like you. He laughs just like you. His facial expressions are just like yours. He acts just like you!" I'm not sure if Jennifer meant that Taylor acts like he's in his mid-30's or if I act like I'm four years old!

Is my goal for Taylor to be a clone of myself? No. Is it his goal to be just like me? No. He doesn't come downstairs in the morning and say, "OK, Daddy, let's get with the program. What aspects of character development are we working on today? I want to see changes in these areas!"

Our relationship is not goal oriented. It is based on expressing and receiving love. My number one desire for my children is that they will be absolutely sure their father loves them. Catherine and Taylor are very responsive. And it is in this environment that they learn to care about the things Joyce and I care about, to value the things we value.

When Jesus was asked, "What is the great commandment?" He replied, "Love the Lord your God." Paul told the Philippians that his life's focus was "the surpassing value of knowing Christ." The clear teaching of the Bible is that our relationship is with God Himself, not just with rules or ideas about God. This relationship is one of unconditional love and acceptance, the source of our security and significance.

Is the Lord delightful to you?

Several years ago I sat in Moby Gym at Colorado State University listening to a speaker give a talk on enjoying the Lord. He talked about King David's single-minded passion to know God, and how he had found God to be delightful. We looked at Psalm 27:4 where David wrote:

One thing I have asked from the Lord, that I shall seek; that I may dwell in the house of the Lord all the days of my life, to behold the beauty of the Lord, and to meditate in His temple.

The speaker asked a question as he concluded his remarks: "Is the Lord delightful to you this morning?"

As several thousand people filed out of the gym, I stayed. I had to wrestle with that question, because my answer was no!

As I sat there in the nearly empty gym, I had to ask myself, "Why not?" I read my Bible regularly. I prayed. I was involved in many activities for the Lord. He loved me enough to die for me. So why wasn't He delightful to me?

After some intense soul-searching, the truth dawned on me. My attention was focused on my activities, my growth, and what I could do for God. I wasn't focused on Him. I was working hard for Him, but I felt little intimacy in truly knowing and loving Him. So I began to focus on the Lord Himself as the source of joy, motivation, and wisdom in my service for Him. The more I focus on Him, the more delightful He becomes to me.

Let me ask you the same question: Is the Lord delightful to you?

The prophet Hosea gave us a beautiful promise that God will respond when we seek Him:

So let us know, let us press on to know the Lord. His going forth is as certain as the dawn; and He will come to us like the rain, like the spring rain watering the earth (Hosea 6:3).

As we seek God, He has promised to make Himself known to us. He delights in our knowledge of Him far more than in our activities for Him.

It is clear that knowing and loving God involves active participation on our part. We cannot be passive in the relationship. In his outstanding book, *Knowing God* (InterVarsity Press), J. I. Packer writes:

> What, then, does the activity of knowing God involve? Holding together the various elements involved in this relationship ... we must say that knowing God involves, first listening to God's Word and receiving it as the Holy Spirit interprets it, in application to oneself; second, noting God's nature and character, as His Word and works reveal it; third, accepting His invitations and doing what He commands; fourth, recognition, and rejoicing in, the love that He has shown in thus approaching one and drawing one into this divine fellowship.

Relationships are not static. They are constantly in a state of flux, either deepening or weakening. The more we understand and love someone, the more we are able to anticipate the person's desires and responses. And when one is in authority over another (such as in a father-child or teacher-disciple relationship), the one being led tends to take on the characteristics of the leader. In our relationship with Christ, we also have the added dimension of the Holy Spirit's work causing the desires and the character of Christ to overflow in us as we focus on Him. Christ explained this phenomenon in John 7:37, 38:

> Now on the last day, the great day of the feast, Jesus stood and cried out, saying, "If any man is thirsty, let him come to Me and drink. He who believes in Me, as the Scripture said, 'From his innermost being shall flow rivers of living water.' "

This overflow is the life of Christ (His love, wisdom, and power) made real in our lives and made available to others through us. It isn't passive. It doesn't just happen. It is the result of experiencing the Lord's love and strength.

The overflow of Christ's life in us involves both the pleasure of enjoying Him and the responsibility of obeying Him with hard-nosed tenacity in gut-wrenching situations. There are times when we are pleasantly surprised by the Lord's work in and through us. There are times when we are confused, yet persevere in our pursuit of Christ and His will. Both are manifestations of the overflow of Christ. And there are times when we are not aware that we are "being changed into His likeness" but the work of grace is quietly and surely taking place.

The critical first step

If there is no overflow of the Spirit's work in our lives (especially over a long period of time), it is time for soul-searching. Unless our lives are reflecting Christ's character, there is no real godliness or ministry. "Apart from Me you can do nothing," Jesus said (John 15:5). Nothing, that is, of eternal value. Empty activity without spiritual overflow is a meaningless treadmill.

The critical first step is the recognition of our need for Christ, our "thirst" for Him. Then we will "drink" of Him, which results in a spontaneous overflow of His love and character to the people around us.

So we have seen that our ultimate purpose is to glorify God. This is accomplished through knowing and loving Him, and the result is that the very life of Christ overflows from us in godliness, love, and service to others. The fruit of this overflow brings honor to God.

Is all this time and attention to our purpose really important? Aren't we really straining gnats and swallowing camels? No, we are not. Our chosen purpose forms the cornerstone of all decision making and indeed, all relationships. It is a vitally important foundation.

An architectural adage states: form follows function. In other words, the design of a building is determined by its purpose. The blueprints for a large stadium are very different from the blueprints for a three-bedroom house because the purposes of the buildings are so different. In the same way, the patterns and direction of our lives are determined by our purpose.

Why do some people seem to respond easily and experience the love and power of Christ, while others find such an experience much more elusive? Our responses are the product of a complex set of factors, including family background, peer relationships, self-esteem, habits, and perceptions. Some of us come from families in which we were nurtured and loved. We developed a sense of strength and humility. We learned to trust, and we learned to take risks. This family environment provided a model and a launching pad for our Christian experience, and we find it relatively easy to believe that God loves us, that He has a purpose for us, and that we can trust Him.

On the other side of the continuum, others have experienced a much different home environment. They may have faced neglect, manipulation, abuse, alcoholism, drug abuse, divorce, workaholism, or some other dysfunction in the family. To some degree, people from these families learn that you, "don't talk, don't feel, and don't trust."

Fear, hurt, anger, and irritability characterize the lives of people from these families, and perceptions of their parents are often transferred to their perception of God. So instead of enjoying His love and trusting His wisdom and strength, these people use their defense mechanisms to block out pain. Some are driven to prove themselves—to gain a sense of value and win the love of others. Others become passive. They avoid risks in situations and relationships because they're too afraid of failure and rejection.

Stable, objective people tend to see discipleship as a process, often a very slow one. They intuitively know that they can't do everything, so they weigh activities in light of their purpose and their abilities, realizing that they have to say no to some things.

Hurting people tend to either try to do everything immediately, expecting instant growth, or they give up almost before they start because they have no hope to succeed. They either can't say no to anything, or they say no to almost everything.

For some people, following Christ in discipleship is easy because they already believe that God is loving and powerful. Others must first be honest about their feelings and thoughts about Him, and about themselves. Hurt, fear, and anger distort their self-esteem and their view of God.

Bypassing this painful process may seem easier, but it is not the solution. Denying the reality of these hurts will ultimately lead to more compulsiveness or passivity, not spiritual growth and health. The process may be longer, but the Lord can heal the brokenhearted and comfort the afflicted. Being honest with God—and with a kind and understanding friend or pastor who won't give you simple answers—may be painful at first, but it is an important first step.

QUESTIONS

1. *How would most of your friends define their purpose in life?*

2. *How does our culture communicate that success, recognition, and pleasure should be our goals?*

3. *What has been your purpose in life? How has that purpose motivated you?*

4. *How would a clear purpose of honoring Christ affect your relationship with Christ? You relationship with*

others? Priorities? Use of time? Use of money?
Daydreams?

Chapter 4
The Motives Behind
Our Choices

Some people equate honoring God with positive circumstances and pleasant feelings about Him, but the assumption is false. Praise, thanksgiving, and obedience are acts of the will that are not dependent on environmental conditions. Honoring God is a choice that needs to be made in spite of pain and confusion. It is an act of faith in His sovereign, inscrutable, loving character.

A friend of mine, James, is a real estate developer who consistently chooses to honor the Lord, whatever the circumstances may be. And the boom-and-bust cycles of Texas real estate create widely varied circumstances! In six- or seven-year cycles, developers seem to experience the prosperity of a prince, then the depravity of a pauper, then princely success again. One year they make big deals; the following year they may scratch and claw to keep those deals from bankruptcy.

A year or two ago, times were good. James was building apartments and developing subdivisions everywhere but Mars.

Yet when we got together, he didn't want to discuss his business. Rather, we talked about friends with whom he had shared the Gospel of Christ. We talked about helping a missionary. We talked about outreach opportunities at the church.

Today, the economic climate has changed. The bottom has dropped out. Instead of putting together complex deals, James now tries desperately to stay solvent. After visits to his lawyer and tense sessions with banks, he could easily have become preoccupied with his problems. He is, however, still preoccupied with the Lord and with eternal issues.

James has made a conscious choice to honor Christ regardless of the family and business circumstances that come his way. The decisions aren't always easy when details don't go smoothly. But James's commitment to Christ doesn't waver.

If our primary motive is success or appreciation, virtually any obstacle can cause anger and resentment. But if our desire is to honor Christ, nothing can block our goal because we can honor Christ no matter what the circumstances.

Paul's choice

The apostle Paul experienced a range of circumstances that boggles the mind. We often think of Paul being persecuted in a number of ways, but one time his problem was just the opposite. As Paul ministered in the city of Lystra, the crowd was so impressed they thought he and Barnabas were gods:

When the multitudes saw what Paul had done, they raised their voice, saying in the Lycaonian language, "The gods have become like men and have come down to us." And they began calling Barnabas, Zeus, and Paul, Hermes, because he was the chief speaker. And the priest of Zeus, whose temple was just outside the city, brought oxen and garlands to the gates, and wanted to offer sacrifice with the crowds (Acts 14:11-13).

Paul and Barnabas were appalled! They stopped the crowd by telling them about the living God (Acts 14:14-18). Yet only a few days after they tried to offer sacrifice to Paul and Barnabas as gods, the crowds had a somewhat different attitude toward them!

Jews came from Antioch and Iconium, and having won over the multitudes, they stoned Paul and dragged him out of the city, supposing him to be dead (Acts 14:19).

I can imagine how I might have responded to this situation. If a crowd appreciated me enough to consider me a god, I may have corrected their thinking, but I would have enjoyed the recognition. Instead, Paul and Barnabas were deeply grieved, tore their robes, and tried with great intensity to focus the people's attention on the Lord.

Later, when the crowd hated me enough to try to murder me, I would have taken a long vacation to think about my lifestyle and commitments. My mind would have been saying, "This kind of treatment couldn't possibly be God's will! What is the abundant life, anyway?" Yet Paul not only survived, but also continued the ministry God had given him with an unwavering sense of purpose.

While the disciples stood around him, he arose and entered the city. And the next day he went away with Barnabas to Derbe.

And after they had preached the gospel to that city and had made many disciples, they returned to Lystra and to Iconium and to Antioch, strengthening the souls of the disciples, encouraging them to continue in the faith, and saying, "Through many tribulations we must enter the kingdom of God" (Acts 14:20-22).

Paul's clear perception that he would choose to honor Christ no matter what the circumstances provided a sense of contentment. He wrote to the Philippians:

Not that I speak from want; for I have learned to be content in whatever circumstances I am.

I know how to get along with humble means, and I also know how to live in prosperity; in any and every circumstance I have learned the secret of being filled and going hungry, both of having abundance and suffering need.

I can do all things through Him who strengthens me (Philippians 4:11-13).

This kind of commitment to honor Christ in every situation doesn't come naturally for any of us. What comes naturally is the desire to honor ourselves, and that desire doesn't easily change. The Lord has a lot of different ways to get our attention so He can teach us sincere and pure devotion to Christ. Hardship, failure, and the loving confrontation of Christian friends are common means He uses to sensitize us to our selfish motives.

When our purpose is to honor Christ, the awesome power of the Holy Spirit becomes available to us. In a positive, nurturing environment, our desires can gradually become united with His desires and our will with His will.

When we seek success and recognition, God withholds His resources of wisdom, power, and love until we stop living for our own glory. The Lord said, "I will not give my glory to another" (Isaiah 42:8). Are we stronger than God Almighty? Are we smarter than the omniscient Lord so that we deserve praise? In light of the awesome character and majesty of God, it is irrational to seek honor for ourselves. He is worthy. We are not.

Peter wrote:

God is opposed to the proud, but gives grace to the humble. Humble yourselves, therefore, under the mighty hand of God, that He may exalt you at the proper time (I Peter 5:5, 6).

I don't enjoy having anyone angry at me. The prospect of the sovereign Lord of the universe setting Himself against me is more than enough to encourage me to evaluate my motives and turn from my selfishness!

Actually, it is gracious of God to withhold His blessing when our motives are selfish. If He blessed our blatant selfishness, it would only harden us in those selfish attitudes. But when we turn from seeking our own glory, He is usually quick to act on our behalf—even in the earliest stages of our pure desire to honor Him.

Focus on the giver

When I was in the sixth grade, I was interested in hunting and fishing. I scoured every issue of *Outdoor Life* and *Field and Stream*. Stories of hunters being mauled by lions or bears were particularly fascinating to me, and pictures of men in hip waders catching fifty-pound steelhead salmon were translated into my own experience with four-ounce bluegill and an occasional small bass.

I became interested in taxidermy so I could preserve the trophies I planned to kill or catch. In the back of *Outdoor Life* was an ad for taxidermy kits. The small one was $15.95, the medium size kit was $25.95, and the super-duper deluxe kit was $39.95. I scraped my yard work earnings together for a month and went for the big time—the $39.95 kit.

A box arrived a few weeks later. That kit had everything anyone could possibly need to mount any creature ever known. There were bags of preservatives, calipers to measure carcasses, several scalpels, plaster mix, and a host of other stuff. My favorite thing in the kit was the box of plastic eyes. It contained dozens of eyes of various shapes, sizes, and colors for birds, fish, and mammals. It was great—at least for a twelve year old!

At about this time, I wanted to do something special for Mrs. Fleming, my sixth-grade teacher. She was kind and fair to everyone in the class. I liked her a lot, and I considered how I could show my appreciation. A deer head? No, Daddy said I was too young to go deer hunting. Bearskin? No. A big fish? I'd never caught anything bigger than a two-pound bass. Maybe a squirrel? Maybe a squirrel head? Yeah, that would be just right!

I roamed around the neighborhood with my BB gun, but the BB's didn't even faze the squirrels. So I decided to get one the easy way—from the street. For several days I rode my bicycle up and down the street looking for a good squirrel that had been run over by a car, but the ones I found had been . . . well, let's just say they wouldn't work.

Finally, I saw one in front of Mrs. Dean's house. It was in good shape for a little squirrel that had been run over by a one-ton car. I put it in a grocery sack and peddled home as fast as I could go. The basement was my taxidermy shop. The Ping-Pong table was the laboratory.

I thought of how those deer heads at the sporting goods store are mounted on handsome walnut shields. Hmmm, what could I use? Maybe popsicle sticks! I put two down about two inches apart and glued eight sticks across them. Perfect!

And now, to prepare the squirrel. I cut its head off with one of my new scalpels. Then I used a little scoop to clean out its brains and sprinkled some alum in the skull cavity to preserve the head. Then I filled it up with plaster. After the eyes were removed, I waited for the socket area to dry (five or ten minutes, at least) and selected the very best pair of plastic eyes from my kit to glue carefully in place. They may have been fish eyes, but they were my favorite ones.

The head was then attached to a big screw through the back of the Popsicle stick "shield." Hmmm, not quite right. Not enough pizzazz. Perhaps the tail would help. I cut off the squirrel's tail and glued it to the shield so that it hung straight down under the head. That was better, but still it didn't seem quite right.

I remembered that some of the deer heads at the store had hooves attached at the bottom to use for gun racks. What a great idea! I cut the front paws off the squirrel and glued them on carefully. They would be just right to hold toothpicks. Now it was perfect.

Mama helped me wrap my gift very carefully, though it seemed as though she wanted to tell me something. Early the next day, I went to Mrs. Fleming's room and presented her with the treasured gift. I was so excited I was about to pop.

Mrs. Fleming said, "Oh, Pat, how thoughtful! I wonder what this could be?" She opened the box and beheld my hand-crafted vision of loveliness. "Oh . . . oh, my! Well . . . thank you so much! You really shouldn't have." I beamed with joy.

About three weeks later I was reading a booklet that came in my taxidermy kit: *Instructions for Mounting Small Animals*. Page one said, "Carefully take all skin off the animal. Take extra care to remove all of the skin from the head. Soak the skull in a preservative solution. Carefully measure the carcass with calipers so you can reconstruct the exact shape with excelsior and string."

Oh, no! I had left all the meat on the head. All I had gotten out was the brains. And that was three weeks ago. *Yuck!*

The next day was one of the hardest days in my life. I decided I had to tell Mrs. Fleming. Before the first bell rang, I walked slowly into her room with my head down. I said, "Mrs. Fleming, do you remember the squirrel head I gave you?" (As if she could have possibly forgotten!) "I . . . umm . . . well . . . I didn't do it quite right. What I mean is, I didn't get all the meat out and it'll stink." (Did I think she wouldn't have discovered this fact by now?) "Mrs. Fleming," I gulped, "I guess you'll just have to throw it away." There, I'd said it. The ordeal was over.

Mrs. Fleming smiled, put her hand on my shoulder, and said, "I wouldn't throw it away for anything. I appreciate it so much!"

"Really? You mean . . . you mean it doesn't stink?"

"I love that wonderful gift," Mrs. Fleming consoled me.

Years later I realized that she must have let somebody else throw it away so she wouldn't have to lie to me.

My gift to Mrs. Fleming, though imperfect, was given with good intentions and a pure heart. Mrs. Fleming received it gladly, and I really believe, cherished it because of the love behind it. In the same way, God gladly receives our gifts of love and our expressions of obedience even though we later learn that the gift itself was imperfect. God looks at our hearts.

Purposeful thoughts

How can a person know what his true purpose is? It can be difficult to determine, because most of us have a complex set of motives and perceptions about God and about ourselves. We touched on this in the last chapter, but here are some additional clues to knowing one's purpose.

First, what is the stated purpose? Though we may not achieve it every time, our stated purpose is the one we use as a benchmark for decisions. If we do not have a clearly stated purpose, or if that stated purpose is borrowed from someone else and not based on personal convictions, we will be less likely to achieve it. In that case, we are subject to any and all ideas and goals that sound good at the moment.

Unfortunately, most of us have either no stated purpose, a vague one, or one that is not backed by deep biblical convictions. The result is that we believe we must say yes to everything that sounds good. We quickly become tired and confused. And then, sooner or later, depending on the emotional and physical stamina of the person, burnout is inevitable.

A careful analysis of our thought life is a good way to discover our true purpose. What do we think about? What are our secret desires? What will be the effect on us if our dreams are fulfilled? What will be the effect on others? Do we dream of a top position in a corporation or a club? Do we dream of wealth, vacations, and expensive possessions? Do we dream of applause and recognition by others? Are we concerned about advancing God's honor and His kingdom?

Make no mistake. We can be thinking and dreaming of church work, evangelism, or discipleship with the real purpose of self-advancement and recognition. In that case, spiritual activities are only the vehicle for our own selfish purposes.

I am not advocating protracted self-flagellation in this analysis. Even a cursory glance at dreams and desires is effective for all of us who have not become totally blinded in our self-perception. If we are determined to honor God in every circumstance as the Holy Spirit enables and as the Word of God directs, then we must tenaciously cling to that godly purpose despite successes and failures, acclaim and disapproval. We need not only the encouragement of the Scriptures but also an awareness of the insidious deception of our culture. This kind of analysis is often very difficult to do alone because we lack perception and objectivity about ourselves. A good friend can provide honest feedback and encouragement to take the next step.

Another appropriate question to ask at this point is whether or not it is possible to have totally pure motives. The answer is no. Until we die or are raptured, we will daily wrestle with the presence of sin. We will not be totally free from self-seeking motives until we see Him face-to-face.

But this fact is not an excuse to give up on the pursuit of higher and purer motives. Throughout the Scriptures, we are encouraged and admonished to seek God's will and God's honor even though the desire for independence and prestige seems overwhelming. God's Spirit points out impure motives and gives us wisdom to make Christ-honoring choices, strengthening us by His Word so that we can obey in spite of pressure and selfish motives. (Read Galatians 5:16-26.)

Taking an honest look at our motives can be threatening. We may find some desires we don't want to admit. We may
also see fears, pain, and resentment that affect our lives more
than we realized. We may discover that we hold unrealistic
expectations about the Christian life. Being honest isn't easy,
but honesty is a vital part of a strong relationship with God.

We are to listen to the Spirit's prompting, know the
truth of Scripture, and then choose goals that honor the Lord.
The struggle to honor God instead of giving in to selfish desires
is often an intense battle, but it is one we must constantly fight
if we want to hear those delightful words, "Well done, good and
faithful servant. Enter into the joy of your Master."

QUESTIONS

1. *Why is it important to understand that honoring
   Christ is a choice, not just a feeling?*

2. *In what ways can you develop a tenacious commitment to honor Christ—whatever the circumstances?*

3. *What do you daydream about? What do these
   daydreams tell you about your goals?*

4. *How do you think the Lord would respond if you
   decided to honor Him as your first priority?*

5. *Read II Corinthians 5:9. When is ambition evil?
   When is it a Christian virtue? How is godly ambition
   developed?*

6. *Paraphrase the following passages:*

   Matthew 22:36-39   *Psalm 27:4*

   Matthew 13:44-46   *Psalm 73:25*

   Philippians 3:7-10   *Jeremiah 9:23, 24*

Chapter 5
Unmasking Deception In Our Choices

If you have ever been backpacking in a remote area, you know how dark it can be on a cloudy night. With the moon and the stars obscured by cloud cover, you can't even see your hand in front of your face.

My friends Pete and Frank were camping on a night like this in the Smoky Mountains. In the early hours of morning, Pete turned over in his sleeping bag and suddenly heard the bone-chilling sound of a rattlesnake—somewhere very close! He couldn't reach for a stick to fling it away from him; in the dark, he might grab the snake. Both men were terrified. They had to wait for the snake to crawl away or for the light of dawn.

Deception in our lives is like a rattlesnake in the dark. For a long time we may not even realize it is there, and when we do, we may not see it clearly enough to fling it away. It is difficult to catch a rattlesnake in the dark. It is equally hard to deal with deception. In both cases we need light, and even then the task is not an easy one.

There is an obvious and important difference between a rattlesnake and deception. Everyone fears and tries to steer clear of a rattlesnake. But the temptation to live for ourselves is deceptive precisely because it looks so attractive. We are drawn toward it, and yet it is every bit as lethal (spiritually, emotionally, and relationally) as a coiled timber rattler. Our society tends to make certain goals (such as prestige, power, pleasure, possessions, approval, and beauty) look like ultimate purposes. Certainly the media paints a glowing picture and tempts us to choose these as our priorities.

The goal of analyzing is not to point condemning fingers and say that we are "holier than thou." The goal is understanding, not condemnation. We need to get a glimpse of some of the influences in our culture which affect us so strongly. Then we can be more alert and aware of the insidious power of these forces. (For more comprehensive reading on these issues, see Oz Guiness's *The Dust of Death*, Allen Bloom's *The Closing of the American Mind*, and Herbert Shlosberg's *Idols for Destruction*.)

Let's examine several attractions that promise to provide meaning and security, but in reality cause pain and emptiness.

Deception #1: Prestige

"Be number 1!" "Be the best!" "Get the promotion you want!" Whether in business, academics, politics, social settings, or any other arena, we often believe the next plateau will prove that we've made it. And indeed a promotion or an honor feels great for a little while. Then the glamor wears off, we become disenchanted, and we start looking to the next slot up the line.

Every football player from the Pee Wee League to the NFL dreams of winning the Super Bowl. Most would give anything to be the winning quarterback, yet the day after one of Terry Bradshaw's Super Bowl victories with the Pittsburgh Steelers, he said he felt empty. Even the most coveted prizes and positions give only fleeting pleasure.

How many business people work sixty to eighty hours a week, year after year, in order to climb the corporate ladder? As key executives in the company, many try to find fulfillment and purpose—even while neglecting their children and spouse. The heights of business, politics, and society are often scaled on the backs of the people God has given us to love and cherish.

The pursuit of a top position is not confined to secular employment. Think how often someone's worth as a Christian is defined by his or her rank on the organizational totem pole. We realize that others value us on the basis of our position, so we pursue advancement in church and parachurch groups.

When I became involved in a Christian organization in college, I quickly figured out what it took to be respected and to climb in the organization. I got an up-front role and learned to say the right things to the right people. Why? To please Christ? Hopefully there was a measure of that motivation, but I also felt a selfish desire for recognition.

The apostle Paul asked penetrating questions:

Am I now trying to win the approval of men, or of God? Or am I trying to please men? If I were still trying to please men, I would not be a servant of Christ (Galatians 1:10, *NIV*).

We are either servants of Christ or of our own interests. It is my choice whose servant I will be. I need to have the intestinal fortitude to ask myself if my heart is in the right place.

Deception #2: Power

Prestige is the position we hold; power is the influence we have. Obviously they often go hand in hand, but power can have its own insidious character. It is the desire for control and autonomy, the ability to make things happen. Some of us want this authority so much that we make ourselves "big fish in a small pond" so we can exercise our clout.

When I was a staff member on the Campus Crusade for Christ team at the University of Missouri, I thought I knew just how things should be done. I couldn't wait to become a director so I could do things my way.

It wasn't long before I was asked to be the local director at the University of North Carolina in Chapel Hill. After a couple of years as a local director, I started looking toward an area director job. "Then I'll really be able to pull strings and get things done," I surmised. And sure enough, CCC eventually appointed me area director in Texas.

Strangely, the same thing happened in Texas that had happened in Missouri and North Carolina. As I became comfortable with the influence and power of a new position, I began to want the next one up the line, with even more power and influence.

Power is intoxicating. When we are successful and others are influenced by us, the experience perpetuates and deepens the intoxication of power. Opposition doesn't weaken the lust for power. Rather, it strengthens the desire to control and pursue personal goals at anyone's expense.

We can pervert the God-given authority structure of the church that is based on humility and servanthood, the opposite of personal power. God penetrated the core of the issue when He said through Jeremiah to Baruch, "Are you seeking great things for yourself? Do not seek them" (Jeremiah 45:5). Is the exercise of authority for the honor of God or for self-glory? The two are kingdoms apart. The authority to control the lives of others is dangerous, so Scripture teaches that humility must be the primary characteristic of spiritual leadership. J. Oswald Sanders accurately concludes:

> The true spiritual leader is concerned infinitely more with the service he can render God and his fellowmen than with the benefits and pleasures he can extract from life (*Spiritual Leadership*, Moody Press).

Do I want power and control over the lives of others? If so, I need to beware!

Deception #3: Pleasure

Not long ago I helped teach a Sunday school class of four-year-olds at our church. As I sat with several children during a lull in the action, I asked one little girl, "Mary, what did you most enjoy doing during the past week?"

"Skiing at Lake Tahoe," she replied with a rather bored expression.

Mary was not even excited! After I picked my jaw off the floor and collected myself, I thought, *Whatever happened to playing with puppies or eating an ice-cream cone?* The affluence in our culture is staggering. The comforts and pleasures of even middle-class people far exceed any time in history, but we are so quickly bored. We increasingly look for greater excitement and more pleasure.

Most advertisements suggest that the comfort and pleasure provided by their products will make us really happy. Unfortunately, we believe them.

In a survey conducted by "Newsweek on Campus" (March, 1985), college freshmen of 1968 and 1984 rated their priorities regarding two areas: "Developing a Meaningful Philosophy of Life" and "Being Well-off Financially." The survey revealed a dramatic change in students' values in the sixteen-year period. In 1968, 82% said that meaning and purpose was their top priority. But by 1984, only 44% said it was of utmost importance. Conversely, in 1968, only about 40% indicated that making money was important. But by 1984, over 71% said that being financially comfortable was of highest priority.

It's easy for me to point fingers and shake my head at those pleasure seekers, but what about me? Do I spend most, if not all, of my time in the holy huddle of Christian fellowship? Am I so caught up with my own growth and entertainment that I seldom do anything meaningful for Christ's sake? Am I seeking comfort at all costs? Have I become too passive, expecting to be taught and entertained, with little thought of obedience unless it makes me feel good?

The lack of healthy relationships with parents and others is a major factor in the propensity of some Christians to be involved in immorality, spiritual lethargy, and an addiction to visual entertainment. Instead of pursuing healthy fulfillment in these relationships, we settle for empty substitutes which are easier to get.

Fun! Pleasure! Entertainment! These become watchwords—no matter what the cost to us, to our families, to our friends, or to Christ's cause.

Deception #4: Possessions

A major goal of advertising is to produce both customer dissatisfaction and a perceived need for a product. No matter what kind of car you have, what brand of clothes you wear, what style of apartment or house you live in, what toothpaste you use, or how you wear your hair, jewelry, or makeup, you need more! You need better!

Paul instructs us to be satisfied with food and clothing—and he isn't referring to caviar, prime rib, designer clothes, and a vacation house at the beach (I Timothy 6:8-19). No, we are to be content with the amount and quality of food, clothing, and housing it takes to keep us alive and healthy—which is a lot less than we think.

Our society assumes you can't be happy unless you have more and better things, yet Paul said we can be completely satisfied with very little if our affections are centered on Christ. When we allow Him to meet our needs for acceptance so that we no longer feel compelled to achieve recognition, then we break free from the prison of possessions and can begin to give generously. Paul wrote to Timothy:

Instruct those who are rich in this present world
not to be conceited or to fix their hope on the uncer-
tainty of riches, but on God, who richly supplies us
with all things to enjoy (I Timothy 6:17).

Compared to people throughout history or to virtually
everyone else in the world today, you and I are fabulously rich!
No, we may not be as wealthy as the people portrayed in the
ads, but ads are not reality. They create an illusion which
suggests everybody ought to be this way.

Do I need more and better things? Probably not. So I
need to consider a number of questions before I plan any
purchase:

- Do I really need it?
- How would the Lord want me to use this money?
- If I get some unexpected money or if my regular
  income increases, do I use it to better my life-style or
  to increase my giving?
- Am I so trapped in acquiring more and better things
  that I miss the joy of giving?

It is true that God does give us good things, but does He
want us to have so much while many of His people around the
world are in need and while mission agencies are crippled
because of a shortage of funds?

Self-indulgence is not a virtue, but neither is excessive,
legalistic self-denial. We need to develop a healthy balance
between enjoying the gifts God has given us and using those
gifts to minister to others.

Deception #5: Approval

Scott and Betty are friends of mine who are typical of
millions of us. Scott is a likable, hardworking, young bank
officer. Betty is involved with taking care of their two children,
leading a third-grade Sunday school class, and being an officer
in a service club. Both Scott and Betty appear to have it all

together, but they experience constant tension because they depend on the approval of others.

When Scott's boss is pleased with him, Scott is eager to tell Betty and others. But if there is the slightest hint that he could have done better, thin-skinned Scott is deeply hurt. He sulks for hours or even days, making excuses and blaming others for the situation.

When Scott is happy, Betty is happy. But if Scott is sulky, Betty thinks it is her fault. Her withdrawal continues the downward spiral because Scott then feels hurt by his non-supportive wife. They both become introspective, sullen, and withdrawn over seemingly small incidents.

Some people are slaves to their need for approval. They learn to do whatever it takes to gain the approval of others. The clothes they wear, the way they talk, where they live, and the people with whom they associate are all designed to win approval from others.

This goal is really a double-edged motivation. They not only want to experience the pleasure of acceptance, but also desperately want to avoid the gnawing pain of being laughed at, ridiculed, or ignored.

All relationships are characterized by one of four degrees of acceptance and rejection. These levels can be described by a typical statement which exemplifies the type of approval:

1. Total rejection: "Nothing you do is ever good enough."

2. Highly conditional acceptance: "You'd better . . . or else."

3. Mildly conditional acceptance: "I like you because . . . ."

4. Unconditional acceptance: "I love you. There is nothing you can do to keep me from loving you."

It is clear that unconditional acceptance is indeed rare and precious. The pain of rejection and pleasure of acceptance are so profound that we have developed elaborate mechanisms to block rejection and enhance the pleasure of others' approval. These mechanisms include manipulating others, being manipulated by others, superficial relationships, defensiveness, being critical of others, exaggerating the truth to impress, and doing whatever it takes to fit in with the peer group. We go to great lengths to gain approval.

Our relentless pursuit of approval does have a solution: the unconditional love, acceptance, and forgiveness of Christ. Though we deserve the bitter wrath of God because of our sin, that wrath has been poured out on Christ instead of us. He paid for it. The apostle John described this love:

By this the love of God was manifested in us, that God has sent His only begotten Son into the world so that we might live through Him. In this is love, not that we loved God, but that He loved us and sent His Son to be the propitiation for our sins (I John 4:9, 10).

The sources of unconditional love and acceptance are Christ Himself and healthy relationships in the body of Christ. We have no need to look further. We can stop the endless and frustrating struggle to win the approval of others. Our consummate desire becomes to please Him whether or not we please anyone else. This attitude is not rebellion and anger; it is a mature independence from manipulation and peer pressure.

If we continue to pursue the approval of people instead of basking in the love and acceptance of Christ, surely it must show that we have a paltry understanding of the magnitude of His grace and the awesome majesty of His character.

Deception #6: Beauty

Our society is bombarded by advertisements telling us hundreds of times each day that we must have this shampoo,

these clothes, that car, her shape, or his muscles to be acceptable. The not-so-subtle intimation is that if we have the right
products, we're in. If not, we are second class at best. The myth
that we can look as gorgeous as movie stars sells billions of
dollars worth of merchandise every year, but that comparison
also causes us to suffer both financially and emotionally.

The urge to have finer clothes, a better shape, a darker
tan, and a smoother complexion is overwhelming for some
people. But no matter how much we have or how beautiful we
are, it's never enough. Wealthy and beautiful people are often
miserable, afraid they will lose their money and good looks—
their only basis of self-worth.

The lengths that people will go to impress others are
humorous. The book, *Surface Chic* (James Charlton, Avon) is a
tongue-in-cheek treatment of wealth. Among other things, it
contains some paper watch faces that simulate an $11,000
Corum watch. You can cut these out and paste them on your
$11 watch. Your friends will be impressed with both your good
taste and your great wealth. That's surface chic!

How much time, money, and energy do you spend on
how you look? Is it wise stewardship of those resources?

The institution of the media

Deceptions are promulgated and reinforced by some of
the most prominent institutions in our society—the electronic
media. The impact of the electronic media on our culture can
hardly be underestimated. Its force is even more amazing when
we realize that the mass media of radio, television, and videos
are relatively recent phenomena. Radio became widespread in
the 1920's and 30's, and television's influence didn't become
widespread until after the early 1950's. The video market has
only sprung up in the past few years.

The major dangers of television and video lie in the
value systems reflected in the programming, and in the impact

of the media themselves. In the early days of television almost all programs were either educational or news-oriented. As entertaining programs gained popularity in the 50's, the programming encouraged audience reflection by twists in plots and subtleties in the characters.

Programs today, however, seem to use much greater amounts of sex and violence to gain and hold the viewing audience. Subtleties and reflection have been lost to primal impulses for power, pleasure, beauty, and prestige. (In my opinion, the last vestige of intellectual credibility in network programming died out when "Rockford Files" was canceled a few years ago.)

Mesmerized

As poor as the programming has become, the impact of the medium itself is just as harmful. Marshall McLuhan, television critic and social analyst, has said, "The medium is the message." I wondered exactly what he meant until I saw my son, Taylor, sit mesmerized in front of the television—no matter what was on. It doesn't matter whether he's watching _Sesame Street_, a nature program, or the news, he sits in his same trance, oblivious even to chocolate chip cookies baking in the kitchen. He becomes so absorbed in the TV show that I literally have to shake him to get his attention. It is frightening.

The medium is indeed the message because the medium transcends program content. Television, by its very nature, robs people of mental energy and meaningful interaction. It puts them in a passive, entertain-me state of mind that is addictive. The more a person watches, the more his faculties of reflection and interaction are dulled. It is easy to watch one more program, then another, and another, and then go to bed.

We don't let Taylor watch much television. It may be a cheap baby-sitter momentarily, but it is expensive if it impedes his mental, emotional, and social development.

Today's music and video programming have justifiably come under attack because of their blatant passion for power and pleasure. In a report on how the media is affecting young people, *U. S. News and World Report* (October 28, 1985) wrote:

Day and night, America's youth are enticed on a world so violent, sensual and narcotic that childhood itself appears to be under siege . . . . Meanwhile, studies show that teenagers listen to an estimated 10,500 hours of rock music between the seventh and twelfth grades alone, just 500 hours less than the total time they spend in school over twelve years.

Rock 'n' roll aimed specifically at this teen market are songs such as "Suicide Solution," "Necrophiles," and "Dancing in the Sheets." Lyrics are explicit. Prince sings a tribute to incest in "Sister."

Video images are just as lurid—even though one quarter of the nationwide audience for MTV is under fifteen. A video by Frankie Goes to Hollywood portrays a rape in a gay bar. One by Duran Duran simulates a lesbian encounter. Critics count eighteen acts of violence in each hour of videos. A survey at the University of Georgia found half of all women in videos provocatively dressed— "presented as upper-class sex objects for lower-class males."

Television violence is so pervasive that the average high school student by graduation day has seen 18,000 murders in 22,000 hours of television viewing—that is, twice as many hours as are spent in the classroom.

As we become more passive, our entertainment needs to become more extreme to satisfy us. It is certainly not wrong to enjoy a good movie from time to time. Legalistic self-denial is not a virtue, but we need to be wise about what our minds dwell on.

What do these staggering statistics mean? Simply that we must be careful how we allow the media to influence our thinking. We may not watch the worst of the TV shows and videos, but what do we watch for relaxation? What values are communicated in the programs we watch and the music we listen to? Are we beginning to believe that comfort, beauty, and success are the ultimate goals in life? That we can and should have all we could ever want, and that all of our difficulties should be completely solved with a happy ending within the confines of a thirty-minute show? That adultery and violence are acceptable in certain situations?

How much time do we spend sitting passively in front of the tube while our minds and relationships atrophy? Will those millions of people who do watch the most lustful and brutal videos become the decision-making adults of tomorrow? God help us.

Other institutions like business, government, and education also propagate a man-centered message where prestige, approval, and comfort are to be pursued at any expense. They, too, have a profound effect on us. These institutions are not as immediate or direct as the media, but they undergird and shape the message that the media presents.

Deception must be exposed to be battled. Once it is exposed, we can see its implications in our lives and replace it with God-given biblical purposes and values. In the next three chapters we will examine three primary counterfeit purposes that are the natural implications of deceptive, man-centered, selfish values.

QUESTIONS

1. *Answer these questions which relate to each section in this chapter:*

Prestige—Are you eyeing the next position of honor in your academics, business career, or social standing?

Power—Do you want to control the lives of others?

Pleasure—Do you spend too much time in the holy huddle of Christian fellowship? Are you so caught up with your own entertainment that you seldom do anything challenging for Christ's sake?

Possessions—Are you so trapped in acquiring more and better things that you miss the joy of giving? Does God want you to have so many good things while others around the world are in need?

Approval—Do you value the conditional approval of other people more than the unconditional love of Christ? If so, what are some of the effects in your life?

Beauty—How much time, money, and energy do you spend on your appearance? Is this wise stewardship of your resources? Why or why not?

The Media—List ways that you are affected by the media. Be specific about each one.

2. Pick up any popular magazine or watch any TV program and identify the message of each ad. How does the ad communicate that the product or service will provide prestige, pleasure, power, beauty, approval, or some combination of these?

3. Read Matthew 16:21-27. List some of God's interests. Then list some of man's interests. What do you think it means to "deny yourself" and to "lose your life"?

How can the judgment in verse 27 motivate us to pursue God's interests instead of our own?

Chapter 6
Problems with Pleasure Seeking

By late 1944, the war in the Pacific was well in hand for the Allies. The Japanese Imperial Navy had been virtually obliterated in the Battle of Leyte Gulf. General MacArthur had 101,365 men ashore in the Philippines. The situation in Europe, however, was far different. Fighting hedgerow to hedgerow, Patton's tanks and the Allied Armies slowly worked their way across France, meeting stiff resistance from Hitler's Germany. The Allies in Europe needed support and supplies, but these were being diverted to another part of the world.

China, which had been the scene of fierce Japanese aggression, was no longer a major military concern, yet Generalissimo Chiang Kai-shek still demanded support for his beleaguered government. Inflation was a major problem for Chiang. Since the outbreak of the war, the consumer price index had risen an incredible 17,400%. For Americans in China, the official exchange rate was intolerable. It cost $10,000 in 1944 dollars to build an outhouse!

To finance such inflation, Chiang depended on massive amounts of paper currency which had to be airlifted by American planes over the Himalayas. This paper currency kept the government alive, but the decision to continue to prop up Chiang's government (which fell to the Communists soon after the war) came at a high price.

Some historians suggest that if the planes used to transport currency for Chiang had been sent to Europe instead, the Allies would have had the air support they desperately needed. Perhaps they would have been able to drive through Germany to the Russian border before the Red Army could capture Eastern and Central Europe.

Those countries would have been under American, British, and French jurisdiction instead of the totalitarian heel of the Soviets. The Iron Curtain would be on the Soviet border, not in Central Europe. The decision to continue to provide needless aid to Chiang had a monumental impact on the history of Europe and the world (*In Search of History*, Theodore White, Warner Books).

Wrong goals have devastating effects on us, too. They involve us in intense, but ultimately fruitless activities that affect our values, relationships, and destiny. The lure of deception leads us to wrong goals—counterfeits of the goal God has given us.

The counterfeit goals of pleasure, success, and approval promise security and purpose, but they cannot deliver on their promise. The counterfeit goals become more obvious when they are juxtaposed next to our biblical purpose. (See the chart on the next page.)

In the last chapter, we saw how several deceptive influences are exalted in our culture. This and the following two chapters will examine pleasure, success, and approval to see how easy it is to adopt these influences as life's compelling purposes. First let's take a closer look at success.

BIBLICAL PURPOSE: TO HONOR CHRIST

FOCUS: Christ

QUESTION: How can I please Christ?

RESULTS: Obedience; thankfulness; godliness; biblical values.

COUNTERFEIT PURPOSES:

PLEASURE

FOCUS: My rights, my comfort, my entertainment.

QUESTION: Does it make me feel good?

RESULTS: Selfishness; moodiness; anger over "violated rights;" seldom satisfied.

SUCCESS

FOCUS: My goals, my performance, my priorities.

QUESTION: What will enable me to meet my goals?

RESULTS: Perfectionism; emphasis on self-improvement; manipulation of people to accomplish goals; seldom satisfied.

APPROVAL

FOCUS: My ability to please others.

QUESTION: What can I do to get people to like me and appreciate me?

RESULTS: Exaggeration to impress people; withdrawal from people or situations when the risk of rejection is too great; succumbing to peer pressure; dress, speech, tastes, etc., are calculated to win the approval of others.

More than a feeling

A preeminent goal in our culture is to maximize pleasure and minimize pain. Comfort and pleasure have been practically deified. People spend an enormous amount of time, effort, and money in order to feel good.

A few years ago, I realized that Joyce and I had not taken a real vacation in the eight years we had been married. Some friends told us what a wonderful time they had on cruises they had gone on, so we got some brochures, talked to the travel agent, and discussed what kind of cruise to take. We had saved enough money to go for a full week on a first-class liner, though in something less than first-class accommodations. Our room was about as big as a tin can with bunk beds and no window.

Our expectations were sky-high as we boarded the ship. The sun was warm, the food was terrific, and the ports of call were enjoyable. But we felt a nagging hint of emptiness. We had thought that the beautiful ship, the convivial people, and the lovely scenery would bring the ultimate in satisfaction, but it didn't. We realized again that only Christ can fill that God-shaped vacuum in each of us. As we lowered our expectations and saw the cruise as a gift from the God who alone gives ultimate joy, we relaxed and enjoyed the trip. The cruise was not the ultimate. Christ is.

Jesus was confronted by a man who wanted his brother to give him some inheritance. In response, Jesus told a parable about a man who sought comfort and happiness:

> He said to them, "Beware, and be on your guard against every form of greed; for not even when one has an abundance does his life consist of his possessions." And He told them a parable, saying, "The land of a certain rich man was very productive. And he began reasoning to himself, saying, 'What shall I do, since I have no place to store my crops?' And he said, 'This is what I will do: I will tear down my barns and

build larger ones, and there I will store all my grain
and my goods. And I will say to my soul, "Soul, you
have many goods laid up for many years to come; take
your ease, eat, drink and be merry." ' But God said to
him, 'You fool! This very night your soul is required of
you; and now who will own what you have prepared?'
So is the man who lays up treasure for himself, and is
not rich toward God" (Luke 12:15-21).

The rich man believed that prosperity, comfort, and
entertainment would give him satisfaction, yet ultimately these
things result in heartbreak and emptiness. The rich man sought
only self-indulgence; enrichment of his own life was not even
considered. Self-indulgence is really compounded selfishness.
The circle of his life had been reduced to a dot.

It is richness toward God—knowing, loving, and
honoring Him—that genuinely satisfies.

In the 1960's and 1970's, our society underwent a driving
urge to "find ourselves," that is, to find fulfillment and meaning
from within ourselves. Either we couldn't find anything or we
didn't like what we found, because we have moved away from
the drive to find ourselves to a goal to numb ourselves. The
intense pursuit of self-revelation has declined considerably.
Today, we are more concerned with being entertained than
finding meaning. We desire comfort more than values.

The Christian movement of the 60's and 70's was a
reflection of those radical times. Christians had intensity and
direction. They were radicals for Christ. Sadly, Christians of
the 80's tended to be a reflection of their self-indulgent times.
With few exceptions, we were more concerned with our prosperity and pleasure than with the honor and kingdom of Jesus
Christ. Perhaps the 90's will be a decade of renewal.

In its obsession with pleasure and comfort, our society is
also in hot pursuit of peace. The pursuit is not toward an end to
the arms race nor a settlement of armed conflicts. It is far more

personal. It focuses on the freedom from wants and nuisances, on being personally insulated from anything that might not contribute to our happiness. Many Christians have joined this pursuit on the premise that Christ has promised us peace.

Indeed He has! But His promise is qualified by one vital characteristic. He said, "My peace I give to you; *not as the world gives*, do I give to you" (John 14:27, author's italics). The peace of Jesus is not the same as the peace of the world. His peace is a calm assurance based on His care and power, even when we are bombarded with life's problems. Jesus' peace requires sensitivity to God's purpose in life's situations. Worldly peace seeks only to avoid hassles and numb pain.

The urge to be entertained has overwhelmed the need to read and reflect. But the more we are passively entertained by TV shows and commercials that portray a sensual and exciting life-style as normative, the more dissatisfied we become. It takes more and more sensuality and excitement to satisfy us. And the cycle continues.

Sexual Pleasure

When people begin to believe that an exciting, sensual life-style is normal, they give in to their desire for sexual pleasures. Christians are falling into this trap at an alarming rate. Constantly bombarded by input from friends and the media that sex outside of marriage is more than acceptable, they do not have the convictions to obey God.

A recent study shows that by age 19, 80% of the males and 67% of the females in the United States are sexually active. And the age of first-time sexual activity is getting younger. Half of the young men who were sexually active first had intercourse between the ages of 11 and 13! It is estimated that the Christian population does not fare much better. The same study found that about 60% of Christian teenagers are sexually active.

Why do so many people get involved in premarital and extramarital sexual relationships? The basic reason is not a desire for pleasure, but the need for intimacy. Whether motivated by a desire to be accepted by peers or a longing to be close to somebody because a spouse's love has grown cold, promiscuous sex holds the promise of intimacy, warmth, and love. But the promise is a sham. The ultimate results are bitterness, heartbreak, and gnawing guilt. Yet we become blind to these consequences by the lethal combination of active hormones, encouragement of friends, and media misrepresentation.

Whether single or married, we must fortify ourselves with biblical convictions and filter out untruths as much as possible. We should not forget that we will stand before Almighty God to give an account of each thought and action.

We must not take the prospect of promiscuity lightly. Its consequences demand definitive action. Paul admonished Timothy: "Flee from youthful lusts, and pursue righteousness, faith, love, and peace, with those who call on the Lord from a pure heart" (II Timothy 2:22).

A use for leisure

Self-indulgence in our culture is increasingly revealed by a preoccupation with leisure. The purpose of leisure is misunderstood by the Christian community. We, along with the rest of society, tend to use leisure to deaden the pain of empty lives. We use it to escape.

Leisure is given to us by God for several reasons, but escape is not one of them. Leisure (whether reading, skiing, swimming, carpentry, or whatever) gets us out of a regular routine so we can recharge our emotional, physical, and spiritual engines. The change stimulates creativity. Physical exertion increases stamina.

Some of us are so driven to earn our acceptance with God and with others that we feel guilty when we try to relax.

As was mentioned previously, some of us are so busy serving others that we don't take time for ourselves. Our problem is not too much pleasure, but too little of it! Even when we try to enjoy ourselves, we do so compulsively. This compulsion is a deeper issue than time management. It is a drive to earn approval and value.

In a loving, supportive, vulnerable environment, driven people can experience the love of Christ. Then the compulsion to accomplish and to please others can gradually subside, and will be replaced by peace, objectivity, intimacy, and fun. We need to realize that rest, leisure, and laughter with friends or family are some of the good gifts our loving Lord gives His children. Accept these gifts gladly, and have fun!

Leisure can also be useful for Christian fellowship and outreach. One businessman I know invites people to play racquetball so he can have a good environment in which to talk about the Gospel after they play. (I wonder if they are more open if he wins or if they win.)

As in every other area of life, we need to bring our leisure under the Lordship of Christ. "How can I please Him?" is a question that applies as much to our recreation as to the other parts of our lives. Two people may participate in the same leisure activities, yet with entirely different motivations. One may enjoy leisure as a gift of the Lord and another may only be seeking to deaden emotional pain. We need to ask ourselves if we are using leisure to actively pursue Christ more and serve Him better. Do we use it to spend quality time with our families, or to get away from them?

Pleasure is elusive. When we pursue it, it usually escapes us. Yet honoring Christ brings tremendous exhilaration and satisfaction in seeing Him at work through us.

Dr. Butch Bradly is an outspoken Christian professor at Texas A&M. On his office wall hangs a poster with a message: "Happiness is wanting what you have; not having what you want." The advertising giants on Madison Avenue wouldn't appreciate that statement, but Christ would.

QUESTIONS

1. *Is pleasure a primary goal for you? In what ways? What are several common ways we make pleasure our goal?*

2. *What are the results of making pleasure a primary goal?*

3. *How can you develop a biblical appreciation for God's peace and a conviction not to seek pleasure as your goal?*

4. *Reread Luke 12:15-21. What did the rich man seek? Why was he a fool?*

Chapter 7
When Success Breeds Failure

In 1923 a very important meeting was held at the Edgewater Beach Hotel in Chicago. In attendance were nine of the world's most successful financiers: the president of the largest independent steel company, the president of the largest utility company, the president of the largest gas company, the greatest wheat speculator, the president of the New York Stock Exchange, a member of the President's cabinet, the greatest stockbroker, the head of the world's greatest monopoly, and the president of the Bank of International Settlements.

Certainly we must acknowledge that these were some of the world's most successful men—at least, in terms of making money. Yet what we revere as success may by much less satisfying or long-lasting than we would expect. Take a look at where these nine men were twenty-five years later.

The president of the largest independent steel company, Charles Schwab, lived on borrowed money for five years before his death and died bankrupt. The president of the largest utility

company, Samuel Insull, died a fugitive from justice—penniless
in a foreign land. The president of the largest gas company,
Howard Hopson, went insane. The greatest wheat speculator,
Arthur Cotton, died abroad, also insolvent. The president of
the New York Stock Exchange, Richard Whitney, was released
from Sing Sing Penitentiary. The member of the President's
cabinet, Albert Fall, was pardoned from prison so he could die
at home. The greatest bear on Wall Street, Jesse Livermore,
killed himself. So did the president of the Bank of International Settlements, Leon Fraser. (From *Pitching Horseshoes*, Billy
Rose, 1948. The meeting at the hotel was a youth congress.)

Choosing to be great

The twelve men who followed Jesus were His best
friends. He spent many days talking with them on their walks
from town to town, and they listened to Him in the evenings
around hundreds of campfires and in homes as He taught about
the unconditional love and forgiveness of God. They watched
Him heal countless people who were sick, blind, or demon
possessed. And on the night before His betrayal, the Master
washed their feet like the lowliest servant. Yet after all this,
they still didn't understand His purpose.

On the night that Jesus knew would be His last with His
disciples, when He undoubtedly would have been comforted by
their kindness and compassion toward Him, they instead had
an argument about which of them would be the greatest. Christ
took that opportunity to teach a valuable lesson about success
and power:

There arose also a dispute among them as to which
one of them was regarded to be greatest. And He said
to them, "The kings of the Gentiles lord it over them;
and those who have authority over them are called
'Benefactors.' But not so with you, but let him who is
the greatest among you become as the youngest, and

the leader as the servant. For who is greater, the one
who reclines at the table, or the one who serves? Is it
not the one who reclines at the table? But I am
among you as the one who serves" (Luke 22:24-27).

Jesus was about to die for the disciples, yet they argued
about their rank. Jesus explained to them that rank in the
kingdom of God is paradoxically the opposite of rank in the
world. The world strives to be the best, the most, the greatest,
yet Christ taught that we are not to be like that. Greatness in
the kingdom means relinquishing prestige and power. As John
the Baptist stated about Christ, "He must increase, but I must
decrease" (John 3:30).

Our society is obsessed with a drive for success and self-
glory. There is an almost endless deluge of self-help books and
manuals to aid us in our quest for self-improvement. A visit to
any bookstore will provide you with material to help you be a
success in everything from plumbing to acceptance in a sorority
to selling widgets. In virtually every area of life—socially, ath-
letically, academically, professionally, physically, ad nauseam—
we are encouraged to be the best.

Predictably, business fosters this success-at-any-price
mentality. In one leading national company, prospective
employees are told plainly that the company is to have first
priority in their lives over their families and any other interests.

In a report on corporate working practices, Ford S.
Worthy says that promotions are based in large measure on the
sheer amount of time an executive is willing to work each
week. Efficiency is not appreciated as much as long hours spent
in the office. In fact, in a hypothetical case of one man working
forty hours a week who produces exactly the same as a man
who works eighty hours a week, Win Priem of Korn/Ferry says
that nine out of ten companies will take the man who works
eighty hours a week, because he'll be a better example to those
under him. (But I have to wonder: A better example of what?!)

Worthy asserts:

Those who aspire to lofty titles at some companies
have, in effect, two jobs: the job they were hired to
do—figuring out, say, the best way to sell breakfast
cereal—and the job of making sure their superiors
know how fabulous they are at selling cereal, how
swimmingly they get along with everyone on the
cereal team, and how well they will handle the next
job up the career ladder.

The long hours it takes to accomplish such feats eat away
at every other priority in our lives.

Cause and effect

There is always a price to pay for priorities. The question
too often unasked is whether the price is worth the reward.
The price paid for success in terms of strained family relationships, divorce, tension, and depression is exceptionally high. Is
it worth it?

In a report on workaholics, industrial psychologist David
Sirota explained, "A normal healthy person has three aspects
to life: work, play, and love. Spending hour after hour at work
is a psychological problem. When self-esteem is based entirely
on work performance, every little ripple at work has enormous
consequences."

What is real success, anyway? According to the Bible,
true success is knowing, loving, and serving God. Elmer
Lappan, former staff member with Campus Crusade, defined
success this way: "Success is finding out what God wants you to
do, and then doing it with all your heart."

If you make millions of dollars, become an officer in a
corporation, and buy expensive cars, houses, and vacations,
what will the price tag be?

The preoccupation with self-improvement has also
penetrated the church. When I was a new Christian, I heard

several speakers teach that my purpose should be "to be like Christ" or "to be conformed to the image of Christ."

Character development sounded good to me, so I adopted that purpose as a personal goal. But through the years as I have studied the subject, I have come to a different conclusion. Because the stated goal of "becoming like Christ" is so prevalent today, we need to examine it carefully.

Two passages are used to substantiate this perspective:

> We all, with unveiled face beholding as in a mirror the glory of the Lord, are being transformed into the same image from glory to glory, just as from the Lord, the Spirit (II Corinthians 3:18).

> For whom He foreknew, He also predestined to become conformed to the image of His Son, that He might be the first-born among many brethren (Romans 8:29).

Yet these passage do not teach that transformation should be our ultimate goal in life. Rather, it is the by-product of focusing on Christ. At some future time, we will be transformed into Christ's likeness. That transformation is not our preeminent goal now; it is promised to us at the second coming of Christ. Yes, there is certainly a measure of transformation in our lives now, but it is faltering and incomplete. At some future time our transformation will be instantaneous and complete.

Two additional passages shed light on this future transformation:

> Beloved, now we are children of God, and it has not appeared as yet what we shall be. We know that, when He appears, we shall be like Him, because we shall see Him just as He is (I John 3:2).

> Our citizenship is in heaven, from which also we
> eagerly wait for a Savior, the Lord Jesus Christ; who
> will transform the body of our humble state into con-
> formity with the body of His glory, by the exertion of
> the power that He has even to subject all things to
> Himself (Philippians 3:20, 21).

Numerous other passages clearly explain that our purpose is to know, love, and honor Christ (see Chapter 3), yet
many people insist that character development is the ultimate
purpose of our lives. Could it be that preoccupation with
growth and character development is the worldly desire for self-
improvement clothed in Christian trappings?

Fixing a focus

I soon discovered that focusing on spiritual growth and
character development quickly leads to introspection. When
that was my purpose in life, I was constantly analyzing my
progress: "Am I growing?" "Am I changing?"

We live in an instant society, but spiritual growth is
often painfully slow. The desire for quick, measurable, obser-
vable change often supersedes reality. Then discouragement or
subtle self-deception sets in. We either become disenchanted
that we aren't improving fast enough, or worse, we try to con-
vince ourselves and others that we are growing and developing
faster than we really are.

If we continue to dwell on character development, our
only recourse is to become even more introspective to find
elements of growth so we will feel better. We also need to find
sin (even where there is none, sometimes) and root it out so we
can get on with the growth and development we value so
highly. Morbid introspection is the scourge of many sincere
Christians who believe that character development and
spiritual growth are the purpose for life.

But growth and development should be more or less spontaneous, supernatural by-products of one who is growing in his love for Christ and appreciation of his forgiveness in Christ. Peter taught this freeing truth in II Peter 1:5-9:

> For this very reason also, applying all diligence, in your faith supply moral excellence, and in your moral excellence, knowledge; and in your knowledge, self-control, and in your self-control, perseverance, and in your perseverance, godliness; and in your godliness, brotherly kindness, and in your brotherly kindness, love. For if these qualities are yours and are increasing, they render you neither useless nor unfruitful in the true knowledge of our Lord Jesus Christ. For he who lacks these qualities is blind or shortsighted, having forgotten his purification from his former sins.

As we focus on our "purification from former sins," we are reminded of our need for the unconditional love and forgiveness of God. There is no room for pride here! In a spirit of humility we then seek to obey the One who has rescued us. Growth inevitably follows.

Our affection and attention is then set on God's character more than on our growth and development. The desire to obey Him out of a sense of gratitude grows within us. It is in that context that we are commanded to emulate His love (I John 4:9-11), His forgiveness (Colossians 3:13), and His holiness (I Peter 1:15).

Even though we are commanded to be like God in certain attributes, we cannot copy Him perfectly. Indeed, to imagine that we can be compared favorably with God is to be deluded about His awesome, infinite perfection and the humble state of mankind. An accurate perception of the power and love of God quickly leads us to a realization of our unworthiness before Him and a deeper appreciation for His compassion and love. That's what grace is all about!

Those who have caught a glimpse of the awesome character of God experience the shock of how little they have progressed and how unlike God they are. Isaiah declared, "Woe is me, for I am ruined! Because I am a man of unclean lips, and I live among a people of unclean lips; For my eyes have seen the King, the Lord of hosts" (Isaiah 6:5). Ezekiel and the apostle John both fell down before the Lord because they were overwhelmed by His majesty. When Christ demonstrated His power over nature by enabling fishermen to catch a large quantity of fish when they had been unable to catch even one, Peter fell at the feet of Christ and exclaimed, "Depart from me, for I am a sinful man, O Lord!" (Luke 5:8).

The better we understand the Lord's characteristics (both communicable, such as love and compassion, and non-communicable, such as majesty and omniscience), the more we will experience pure and simple devotion to Him. We will live to please and worship Him. We will be less concerned about our own growth. And we will certainly not be so audacious to think that we are like Him (or that He is like us). We will be gripped by the differences, not the similarities.

While it is not productive to focus on character development, we *are* told to imitate God. Paul wrote to the Ephesian believers, "Be imitators of God, as beloved children" (Ephesians 5:1). The key phrase here is "as beloved children." There is a stark contrast between a child wanting to be like his father and having a self-indulgent desire for personal improvement.

The child imitates his father, who loves him deeply and who is a strong protector and provider. A child has no thought of self-improvement. He simply acts like, and learns to think like, the one who is his source of constant security and joy.

When Taylor learns to enjoy baseball as much as I do, or when Catherine enjoys ballet and painting as much as Joyce does, it will not be because their supreme goal is to be like us. They will simply be acquiring our values and tastes in a more-

or-less loving, supportive environment. They imitate us consciously or subconsciously because they know they are dearly loved children.

Conversely, the preoccupation with self-improvement is like Satan's proud pronouncement of independence from God and his desire to receive glory instead of God: "I will ascend above the heights of the clouds; I will make myself like the Most High" (Isaiah 14:14).

The child wants to imitate his loving father, and Satan wants to imitate God, but their motives are kingdoms apart. They both want to imitate one who is greater, but one does it out of love and appreciation, the other out of a self-seeking desire for power and honor.

We must not underestimate the self-serving effects of our society on our desire for self-glory. Jeremiah wrote: "The heart is more deceitful than all else and is desperately sick; who can understand it?" (Jeremiah 17:9) We need to examine our motives. Are they soundly biblical and honoring to Christ alone? Paul's warning is again appropriate:

I am afraid, lest as the serpent deceived Eve by his craftiness, your minds should be led astray from the simplicity and purity of devotion to Christ (II Corinthians 11:3).

Please don't misunderstand me. Character development is not wrong. Indeed, we are commanded to imitate Christ and to grow in grace and knowledge. Character development is one of God's goals for me, but it should not become the ultimate goal. As an ultimate goal, it has been prostituted in our culture to serve self-glorification and self-honor.

I have often heard people make decisions with the statement: "It will help me grow." The statement is actually self-centered and self-seeking. While growth may indeed be one of the by-products of honoring Christ, it will most likely occur as a result of an arduous period of obedience.

A personal goal of growth and character development often limits us to what we can accomplish on our own, which hinders God's power. God will not share His glory with another, so He withholds His power from the one who seeks his own growth, his own success, and his own glory.

QUESTIONS

1. *Think of three men or women (you know fairly well) whom you consider to be successful. What are some characteristics of their lives, both good and bad?*

2. *Why do we idolize people who are successful in one area of their lives while the other areas are falling apart?*

3. *Why are goals such as "spiritual growth" or "becoming like Christ" inappropriate? What are some results of these goals? Why do they seem so attractive?*

4. *Reread Luke 22:24-27. How does Christ define greatness? How does the world define greatness? Is it difficult to have a servant's heart in our culture? Why or why not?*

Chapter 8

Driven by the Desire for Approval

Glenn was a bright graduate from Texas Tech with a degree in civil engineering. He impressed the executives of a firm in Illinois, and was offered an excellent job with a starting salary of $30,000 a year.

But within four months, Glenn's life was unraveling. He was $8,000 in debt. All he could afford to eat was cereal three times a day. The power company came to turn off his electricity and the bank repossessed his new car. Glenn was scared. He was out of control. His compulsive spending had rapidly snowballed into a catastrophe. He despaired, "I have nothing left." But what caused his predicament?

Glenn's girlfriend, Betty, told him during his senior year that she wanted to marry a man with a nice car, a fine house, and plenty of money for clothes, travel, and everything else she wanted. Glenn wanted to marry Betty, so he determined to meet her expectations. But he could never do enough. Every time she saw something she wanted, she made a not so subtle comment that if he loved her, he'd get it for her. And indeed, he tried—at least until the loans were called at the bank.

Glenn's actions may seem ludicrous, but the fear of rejection can drive people to do some strange things.

At the mercy of others

Most of us do not realize to what extent our lives are dictated by the desire to be accepted and a corresponding fear of rejection. We wear clothes we think other people will like. We try to say things that others will think are clever, cute, or profound. We buy things and attend functions to impress others.

Imprisoned by the whims of others, we become easily manipulated. Any hint of outright disapproval or imagined displeasure is so painful to us that we do whatever it takes to avoid it. Like Glenn, we become puppets whose actions are dictated by the desires of others. And we begin to manipulate others to do what pleases us.

The paradox is this: Even when we succeed in pleasing people, our relief from the fear of rejection is only short-term. Our desire to please others is actually reinforced, and we become further enslaved to people's approval.

Jesus addressed this problem in the Sermon on the Mount. He taught that the temporal reward of pleasing people comes at the expense of far more valuable eternal rewards. He also provided a number of warnings, directives, and promises.

His overall warning is stated first:

Beware of practicing your righteousness before men
to be noticed by them; otherwise you have no reward
with your Father who is in heaven (Matthew 6:1).

Notice the contrast in motives: to be seen by others, or to serve the Father who sees in secret. If we want our activities (in this case, spiritual activities) to be noticed by other people, then the approval and recognition they provide is all the reward we will ever receive. (Also see I Corinthians 3:10-15.)

But if we learn to find satisfaction as we keep our actions secret, the result will be a pure motive before God. The choice is clear: the short-lived approval of fickle people, or the pleasure and reward of God Almighty.

Secrecy is one of the hallmarks of a mature faith. The measure of a person's spiritual virility is not what he does publicly, but what he does privately.

The desire for recognition hinders our relationships with God. In fact, seeking the approval of people may actually prohibit faith in God. Jesus once asked, "How can you believe, when you receive glory from one another, and you do not seek the glory that is from the one and only God?" (John 5:44).

Despite the clear teaching of Scripture, many people continue to crave the approval of others. Perhaps it is because another person's approval is immediate and visible, and because we desperately want to feel loved. God's approval, on the other hand, may seem distant and abstract. We tend to focus on the here and now rather than on unseen, eternal considerations.

This problem becomes evident in our lives in dozens of little ways. I was telling a friend about some phone calls I had made to a man who repeatedly told me, "I really want to give to your ministry, but I can't right now. Call me in a month. I'll help you then." I would call him the next month and he would tell me the same story. This continued for several months.

When I relayed this story to my friend, I said, "I must have called the man nine times!" As I said it, I instantly realized that the number was probably seven, or maybe eight. It *may* have been nine, but why didn't I just say seven or eight? Obviously, I wanted my friend to be a little more impressed with me.

The thought hit me: *Am I not secure enough that I can tell the truth? Do I have to lie to impress people so I can feel good about myself?* I quickly corrected my statement, but I saw the lengths I will go to win others' approval.

The objective here is not to condemn ourselves if we feel
a need for approval. We are looking for understanding and
healing, not guilt. So whenever we realize that we are altering
what we believe, think, say, or do so that others will accept us,
we should stop and ask ourselves why.

Perhaps the reasons are hidden in the past, in our home
environments and the development of our self-concepts. All of
us struggle with the desire to "fit in." Those from relatively
stable home environments tend to develop a strength of heart
and an independence from the oppressive pressure to conform
to others' desires. They believe they are lovable. They can be
fairly objective and honest. They can say no.

But those who have experienced instability at home may
not have this firm foundation in their lives. Neglect, manipulation, role reversals, poor parental modeling, emotional abuse,
and a host of other family maladies leave the growing child
with deep hurts—often including a few that he isn't aware of.

Some people withdraw from others as a defense against
the pain of past or present rejection. Others become virtual
puppets, doing whatever it takes to win the approval of others.
Such people may appear to have their lives in control. They
may in fact be successful and popular, but underneath the
facade of each one is a hurting person. The last thing these
people need is more guilt and condemnation. They need
understanding and the freedom to feel, trust, and grow in an
environment of honesty, love, and acceptance.

Hurting people create countless variations of defense
mechanisms. Most of us practice some combination of healthy,
passive, and compulsive behavior. But hurting people frequently focus on pleasing others to win approval and affection.

Why please people?

Well, then, if we are not to seek approval, is it a virtue to
be obnoxious? Can we just disregard how we come across to

others? No, of course not. Pleasing people is, in fact, a biblical command. But the reason we should please people is not to win their approval. Rather, it is to build up fellow believers (Romans 15:2) and to advance the Gospel (I Corinthians 10:31-33). When we realize that our needs for security and significance have been fully met by Christ, we become free to please others for *their* benefits, not our own.

How can we tell whether we are serving others to win their approval or to honor the Lord? We must consider: Is the service for the glory of God? Is it for the benefit of others? Is there a desire for recognition?

The desire for approval and acceptance is a God-given need. When we allow Him to meet that need in the context of supportive, healthy relationships, we can experience His love, forgiveness, and acceptance. But when look to other people to meet that need, a Pandora's box of problems inevitably ensues.

At this point, it is helpful to look at a summary of glaring contrasts between selfish purposes and purposes that honor Christ.

	SELFISH PURPOSES	CHRIST-HONORING PURPOSES
Luke 12:15-21	Pleasure—"to eat, drink, and be merry"	Richness toward God—whatever the cost (possibly even suffering)
Luke 22:24-27	Success and power—"to be the greatest"	To serve—"become as the youngest"
Matthew 6:1-18	Approval of people—"in order to be noticed by men"	Secrecy—The reward of being honored by God

It is foolish for us to go with the flow and succumb to these tempting but empty deceptions of pleasure, success, and approval. When we understanding both the painful consequences of giving in and the wonderful benefits of honoring Christ, we gain the intensity and tenacity we need to fight the good fight of faith.

Seeing clearly through the interference

Mankind was created to love, honor, and serve God. Our proper response is to worship Him, to live for Him, and to depend on Him. However, sin corrupts our perception of God, and Satan blinds our minds (II Corinthians 4:4).

We get a clear insight on the devil's schemes in Isaiah's account of what many scholars believe to be a reference to Satan's downfall. It is a five-fold assertion of self-dependence and self-glory:

> How you have fallen from heaven, O star of the
> morning, son of the dawn! You have been cut down
> to the earth, you who have weakened the nations!
> But you said in your heart, "I will ascend to heaven; I
> will raise my throne above the stars of God, and I will
> sit on the mount of assembly in the recesses of the
> north. I will ascend above the heights of the clouds; I
> will make myself like the Most High" (Isaiah 14:12-14).

Satan is called "morning star" and "son of the dawn." Both titles refer to his position before his rebellion against God when he was Lucifer, the angel of light. The five "I will" statements outline Satan's plan to exalt himself above all creation, rivaling even God Himself. Satan's culminating assertion was, "I will make myself like the Most High."

C. Fred Dickason comments in his book, *Angels: Elect and Evil* (Moody Press):

> This is the climax of all self-assertion and defiance
> of God! Why did Lucifer choose this title among all
> the titles of God? Because it refers to God as the
> possessor of heaven and earth. Satan wants to be in
> control, to be honored, to be the greatest.

It is noteworthy that Satan used the same concept of independence and honor as he tempted Eve. He promised that if she ate the forbidden fruit, she would "be like God" (Genesis 3:5). Many are led astray by the same temptation each day.

An insidious form of this deception is present even in certain Christian circles today. Some leaders teach that God's primary purpose for us is prosperity, happiness, and success in every area of life. People who believe such fallacious doctrines expect that God will always make them comfortable, healthy, and wealthy. If He doesn't, they must not have enough faith. They are taught that God is honored primarily by our prosperity and that suffering is a sign of a flaw in the person.

One time I began a study of faith, primarily in the Gospels. I was intrigued by the faithful dependence demonstrated by such people as the centurion (Matthew 8:5-10) and Jairus (Matthew 9:18-30). I prayed: "Lord, teach me to depend on You more." It seemed harmless enough at the time.

But shortly afterward, I began experiencing a number of financial problems, failures in my job, disappointments over missed opportunities, and a series of sinus infections that I couldn't shake (even with a new, high-powered antibiotic that kills everything that even comes close to your body).

My mother, who was visiting us from Georgia, fell down our stairs and broke her kneecap. She had to have surgery and then camped out in our dining-room-turned-hospital (since we don't have a downstairs bedroom). My wife's mother, who had terminal cancer, steadily grew worse and soon went to be with the Lord. We had a small fire in one of our bedrooms.

When I asked the Lord to teach me to depend on Him, I didn't have all these problems in mind! I could have used a little health, wealth, and prosperity along the way! My life has included some times of anger and despair, yet the presence of God has become more of a reality to me. I have had to look again at what is really important. And a sense of thankfulness and peace has begun to take the place of anxiety. It hasn't been easy, but the Lord is indeed teaching me to depend on Him.

That elusive sense of satisfaction

Much of the emotional pain and even many of the physical problems we suffer may be the result of reaping what we sow. They are consequences of living in the pressure cooker of suppressing our hurts, fears, and anger, and of nurturing wrong purposes. The stress generated by the drive to succeed, to achieve status and comfort, and to be appreciated by others is immense. If our goals are wrong, we can never let our guard down! Nothing we accomplish satisfies us for long. We sense a compelling need to work a little harder, be a little more clever, accumulate a little bit more—then we'll be satisfied.

But most satisfaction is elusive. John D. Rockefeller, one of the wealthiest men in the world, was asked, "What would it take for you to be satisfied?" He responded, "Just a little bit more. Just a little bit more." Coupled with the pipe dream that complete satisfaction is just around the next corner is the nagging fear of failure and the disapproval of people. The lust for more and the fear of less is a double-edged sword.

The results of wrong purposes vary depending on personality and circumstances, but generally they provide little joy, peace, or contentment. We experience no joy of reflection because it is too painful to admit the truth. We are too busy for it anyway! We experience mood swings, shallow relationships, manipulation by (and of) others, withdrawal, morbid introspection, pervasive guilt, and repressed anger that erupts from time to time. Some people have physical reactions to the constant stress of wrong purposes: chronic tiredness, stomach problems, tension headaches, and many other fairly undefinable ailments.

Self-seeking purposes can be pervasive. The evil one has blinded the minds of people so that they want to please only themselves. Even many Christians, who have been rescued out of Satan's domain by the blood of Christ and who want to please God, continue to be deceived by Satan's schemes.

In a previous era when a similar lust for power and pleasure threatened to overwhelm the cause of Christ, historian Alexis De Toqueville wrote, "Each citizen is habitually engaged in the contemplation of a very puny object, namely himself."

There is One far more worthy of attention and affection. In the next chapter we will examine how Christ has fully met our desperate need for security and significance.

QUESTIONS

1. *Have you said or done some things in the past week to impress other people? What were they?*

2. *How do you respond when people disapprove of you? Give examples.*

3. *How would a deeper understanding of Christ's unconditional love and acceptance affect:*

    • *Your self-concept?*

    • *Your relationship with Him?*

    • *Your relationship with your family?*

    • *Your relationships with your friends?*

4. *Read Luke 16:14-15.*

    What does it mean to "justify yourselves in the sight of men"? Why is it detestable to God? Are you ever guilty of this practice?

5. *Read Luke 14:7-11.*

    Do you try to take the place of honor when you are with other people? What would be the results in your life if you were willing to take the last place?

Chapter 9
Making Decisions
Based on an Accurate
Concept of God

On the first day of class in a major seminary, the theology professor walks into the room, looks at the students and asks simply, "What is God like?" Then he turns and looks out the window while the students give stock answers like: "God is love." "God is omnipotent." "God is omniscient." And on and on. After the clichés have been exhausted, there is a long, awkward lull. The professor now has the students' rapt attention. Knowing that, he turns to the class and says slowly, "God . . . is not like anything!"

The professor is correct. And since God is not like anything, it is difficult for us to put together an accurate mental picture of His nature and His desires for each of us. God cares about our actions and our choices, but His concern doesn't end there. He also cares about our motivation. What we do is only half the battle; the why also needs to be answered.

There are many good, biblical reasons to obey Christ: His love for us, the fact that sin is destructive, the prospect that

God will discipline us if we continue in a habit of sin, the knowledge that God's commands are for our good, to set a godly example for others, to receive eternal rewards, and so on.

But as we have seen, there are also several impure and selfish reasons we may choose to do the right thing: to meet a personal standard of righteousness (and therefore avoid the guilt of not "living right"), to please others by our goodness, or perhaps even to cause God to feel obligated to bless us. These kinds of reasons do not constitute obedience to God at all. They represent denial, self-righteousness, self-glory, or greed.

Understanding God's love and power

No Christian would dispute that Christ is worthy of our love and obedience. It is a given theological assumption. So the question to be answered is whether or not we understand to some extent just *how much He loves us and how great His power is to those who love Him.*

As we begin to understand and experience God's love and power, we are able to serve Him with pure motives. We have no room for self-promotion if we are overwhelmed with what He has done for us. Office politics, the need to be visible, the demand for credit to be given where credit is due, will all fade away as we respond to the love of God. Nothing else will matter except that we are pleasing to Him.

Some people perceive God as a sort of cosmic cop, like a highway patrolman with a radar gun, waiting to catch us moving faster than we should. This misguided perception results in an unhealthy fear of God, a loss of intimacy with Him, and an emphasis on our obligation to do everything just right. It is true that God hates sin, but it is also true that He paid the price for our forgiveness. He loves us!

Others believe that God is loving, but unavailable—like a father always away on a business trip. Consequently, we feel left on our own and may compensate with self-reliance. God is, indeed, transcendent and awesome, but we need to remember He is also present and compassionate.

Some of us believe that God's desire is for us to be completely happy all the time. We envision a heavenly Santa Claus who will give us virtually anything we want. When He doesn't meet these unrealistic expectations, we experience disillusionment and anger. God is gracious and abundantly generous, but He has much higher goals than our self-indulgence.

Still others believe that a relationship with God is strictly cause-effect—if we do our part, then He is obligated to respond. But we cannot make deals with Him. God will not be boxed in that way. Yes, He answers prayer and He is true to His promises, but not at the expense of His reputation or our perception of Him. We cannot make the sovereign, Almighty God obligated to us.

Intimacy with God?

So what is God like? Why is Christ worthy of our love and dependence?

An accurate perception of the deep love and awesome power of Christ is found at the cross. There, the wrath we deserve was propitiated (satisfied) and we received forgiveness and unconditional love. But we do not worship a Savior who is a corpse. Christ was raised from the dead in an awesome display of the power of God (Ephesians 1:19-23).

In Revelation, written by the apostle John, he describes a picture in heaven of three groups giving praise to the risen, living Christ because He is worthy of it. Read the following passage and notice the increasing magnitude of those who praise Him, as well as the content of their worship:

> The four living creatures and the twenty-four elders
> fell down before the Lamb. Each one had a harp and
> they were holding golden bowls full of incense, which
> are the prayers of the saints. And they sang a new

song: "You are worthy to take the scroll and to open
its seals, because You were slain, and with Your blood
You purchased men for God from every tribe and
language and people and nation. You have made
them to be a kingdom and priests to serve our God,
and they will reign on the earth." Then I looked and
heard the voice of many angels, numbering thousands
upon thousands, and ten thousand times ten thousand. They encircled the throne and the living
creatures and the elders. In a loud voice they sang:
"Worthy is the Lamb, who was slain, to receive power
and wealth and wisdom and strength and honor and
glory and praise!" Then I heard every creature in
heaven and on earth and under the earth and on the
sea, and all that is in them, singing: "To Him who sits
on the throne and to the Lamb be praise and honor
and glory and power, for ever and ever!" The four
living creatures said, "Amen," and the elders fell
down and worshiped (Revelation 5:8-14, *NIV*).

Love, praise, and obedience are the natural responses of
those who recognize the true character of Jesus. As we take a
closer look at both the love and the power of Christ, we see
that He is indeed worthy of our love and dependence.

I used to believe that God tolerated me, but I did not
sense His genuine love for me. It was as if I had disappointed an
old friend, and He was obligated out of politeness not to reject
me outright. My relationship with God held very little joy or
intimacy. I resolved to work hard to earn His acceptance, but
after a while I gave up entirely and settled for an arm's-length
relationship.

Some people feel true gratitude for Christ's payment for
their sins, but the risk of vulnerability and intimacy is too
much to bear. The fear of being hurt keeps them at a safe distance from Him. They may interpret painful events in their

lives as signs of God's disapproval or weakness. Perhaps they wanted something badly, but God didn't come through as they had hoped. During such times they must avoid the tendency to look at what they want instead of marveling at the magnificent expression of Jesus' love at the cross.

Remembering God's love and power

The religious leaders of Jesus' day plotted to kill Him. They tried to discredit Him by asking trick questions, but His astute replies gave Him even more favor among the people. Then, as the Passover approached, Judas went secretly to the high priest to arrange a deal. He agreed to betray Jesus for thirty silver coins, a month's wages.

The arrest in the Garden of Gethsemane startled Jesus' disciples. They ran off, leaving Him alone with His captors. In the ensuing trials and hearings, Jesus was subjected to brutal emotional and physical torture.

Witnesses lied about Him. Religious leaders bitterly scorned Him. Roman soldiers spat on Him and beat Him in the face with their version of brass knuckles until He was hardly recognizable. The Roman governor had Him scourged, which took most of the skin off His back as the whip's pieces of bone and metal were driven into the skin and raked across His flesh. Finally, Jesus experienced the epitome of pain and humiliation on the inhumane and excruciating form of torture reserved for the worst of criminals—the cross.

With spikes driven through the wrists and both feet, the prisoner was forced to writhe, shifting his weight from feet to hands and back to the feet again as the pain became unbearable. The process was slow. It usually took two or three days for a person to get so exhausted that he could no longer move to get a breath of air. Suffocation soon followed.

As horrible as this physical pain was, there was even more agony ahead for Christ: the pain of being separated from perfect union with the Father so that He could experience the righteous wrath of God against sin. On the perfect, sinless Christ were placed all of the sins of the entire world.

He made Him who knew no sin to be sin on our behalf, that we might become the righteousness of God in Him (II Corinthians 5:21).

Feeling the separation from His Father and the crushing weight of God's righteous wrath against our sins of pride and self-righteousness, Jesus cried out, "My God, My God, why hast Thou forsaken Me?" (Mark 15:34). It would be the first and last time He would have to experience the torment of bearing our sins and being separated from the Father.

Yet Jesus made it clear that it was His *choice* to go to the cross. He could have escaped the dreaded torture by simply asking the Father for help. He told those who arrested Him:

Do you think that I cannot appeal to My Father, and He will at once put at My disposal more than twelve legions of angels? (Matthew 26:53)

Some people mistakenly envision angels to be chubby, happy babies floating on clouds with bows and arrows. God's angels are powerful creatures, created to honor and serve Him. The Old Testament describes how, on a single night, a lone angel killed 185,000 Assyrians (II Kings 19:35). Jesus said He had more than *twelve legions* of angels (somewhere between 36,000 and 72,000 of the powerful beings) at His disposal—an awesome army!

Adrian Rogers, pastor of Bellevue Baptist church in Memphis, Tennessee, paints a vivid picture of what could have happened at the crucifixion:

In response to mankind brutally mocking and murdering their Lord, it was as if the mighty angels peered over the parapets of heaven with their swords drawn and their teeth clinched, shouting, "Lord Jesus, say the word and we'll slay them all!" But instead,

Jesus looked at those who were killing Him and said,
"Father, forgive them, for they don't know what they
are doing."

Such is the love of Christ. He could have escaped the
torture at any time, but "He endured the cross, despising its
shame" for you and me.

Examples of God's love

A while back I had a large, painful abscess at the end of
my left ear canal. An abscess, like a boil, is very tender, and the
slightest touch around it is very painful. My neighbor, who is a
doctor, said I needed to have it surgically opened so it could
drain and heal. So that night I went to the hospital emergency
room and waited for someone to see me. Finally, a doctor came
in to take a look. She confirmed that it needed to be opened,
and she filled a syringe with novocaine. (Why do they use such
huge needles for such a little place?)

As she repeatedly jabbed in the needle around the swel-
ling, I suspected it was the dullest one in the hospital. When
she was through, I checked her name plate to see if I recognized
the name of some famous sadist. I didn't, but I was in pain!

After a few minutes to let the novocaine take effect, she
put on surgical gloves, washed my ear with betadine, and took
out a scalpel. She put a cloth over my head so that only my ear
stuck out. Her next words were not comforting: "I hope the
novocaine has had time to work." *Zip.* The scalpel cut across
the top of the abscess. No problem there. After some pressing,
dabbing, and a little more cutting, I thought things were pro-
ceeding nicely. Then she started scraping an area where the
novocaine hadn't reached.

I tried to be nonchalant (which means I muffled a
scream). I attempted three times to let the doctor see the desperate expression on my face, but my cloth head covering kept
getting in the way.

It is difficult to be cool when someone is slowly scraping out the inside of your skull with a dull ax—or so it felt. Finally, after several hours (actually about 20 or 30 seconds), she was through. I put my eyes back in their sockets and checked to see if I had swallowed my bottom lip. I then headed home, very glad the experience was over.

The next morning, I was listening to a Christian radio station on the way to work. The speaker was talking about the pain that Christ endured on the cross. As he described the chain of events during the last days of Christ, I compared His pain with the pain I had endured the previous night.

I had novocaine; He didn't. My pain was very localized; His was from head to foot, including emotional and spiritual suffering. Mine was over in a couple of minutes; His lasted hour after hour. Mine was necessary pain at the hands of a person committed to helping me; His suffering was at the hands of those who passionately hated Him. Mine was for my benefit; His was totally for the benefit of others.

The pain I had endured gave me a fresh perspective on what Christ did for me. He endured unspeakable agony that He could have avoided. And He did it because He loved me.

Another excellent illustration of the love of Christ is found in J. Sidlow Baxter's *Going Deeper*. Baxter writes:

Back in the grim old days of slavery, an emaciated Negro waits trembling in a slave market. Soon he is sold to the hardest slave owner who ever curled a whip over the bodies of his cringing victims. The servitude is almost unendurably rigorous; the chastise-ment for default is merciless; the plight of the wretched slave and his fellows is pitiful. One night he attempts escape, but is dragged back, whereupon his gloating owner decides to inflict exemplary punish-ment—a major lashing such as almost always means death to the undernourished slaves. In the morning he is tied naked to the whipping post; the whippers are called; and he is just about to be thrashed before onlooking slaves and several white visitors, when a strange thing happens. One of the visitors, a tall, noble-looking gentleman, exclaims, "Stop; you cannot whip that poor slave so brutally; he will die!" The slave owner, little dreaming what is to follow, glares and retorts, "Then die he shall, unless you, brave sir, will take his punishment." The handsome stranger steps forward. "You have committed yourself," he says to the wicked owner. "Free the slave, and I will take the lashing." He bares his back to the smiters; his body quivers under the lashes; but he endures manfully until the last two strokes, when he sinks to the ground, lacerated, bleeding, exhausted.

There is more to follow, however. Imagine our slave's increasing astonishment when, some days later, he is summoned before his master, who says, "You are my slave no longer. That man who suffered for you has now paid such a price to free you that I cannot keep you any longer. Go. You are free."

Nor is even that all; for on going out the freed slave is intercepted by a messenger from his amazing benefactor, with new clothing and good food, and a message that all the money he can require has been deposited for him at a central bank. But the climax comes when, on enquiring at the bank, he learns the name of his wonderful deliverer. He is a king's son; is incalculably rich; is the freer of many, many, other suffering slaves; is so upright and noble, so strong yet so humble, so unselfish, gracious and kindly, so understanding and individually sympathetic, that all his great household love him, and find him ever more lovable the more they know him.

Well, is it surprising that the consuming passion of
our liberated slave is now to traverse the hundreds of
miles, whatever the hazards may be, if only he may
get to his benign benefactor, fall at his feet, look up
into his face, become his willing bond servant, then
enjoy knowing him, loving him, and serving him
forever? Is it surprising that he wants to be ever in his
noble rescuer's presence, looking into that wise, kind,
gracious countenance, knowing him face-to-face, and
even heart-to-heart?

The freed slave's loving response toward the one who
sacrificially paid for his release is a good example for us. God's
grace has two aspects: it frees us from the bondage of sin, and it
compels us to live for the One who loves us enough to set us
free.

A father's love

The love of God is often communicated in examples of a
father-child relationship. I certainly love my children. It is my
customary bedtime ritual to look at them, fix their blankets, sit
on their beds, kiss them, and pray for them. One night, I
thought, *How wonderful it is that Catherine and Taylor are my
children. I love them so much.* Then the question popped into my
mind, *I wonder if God loves me as much as I love Catherine and
Taylor?* My instantaneous response was, *Heck, no!*

But then my theological self took over and I realized how
wrong I was. In essence, I had concluded that the love of the
infinite, compassionate God, demonstrated plainly by the
sacrificial death of Christ, is inferior to a quite finite and flawed
man's love for his children. Such an assumption is ludicrous!
God's tender and strong love is infinitely greater than mine. No
matter how much I love my children, God's love for me is
obviously far more. I felt both deeply reproved and greatly
encouraged.

God has gone to great lengths to reveal the depth of His love for us. He does not just tolerate us. He loves us with an unconditional, strong, and pure love that only He can offer.

As humanism has deified man and humanized God, it has given us the perception of a puny God who sees our problems but wrings His hands because He can't do anything about them. The Scriptures, however, present a different picture of God. Because of His power and His love, He is worthy of our love and dependence.

Perspective from Isaiah

Many passages of Scripture demonstrate the power of the Almighty God. We could examine creation, the miracles, the resurrection, or doctrinal statements, but one of the most comprehensive passages is Isaiah 40. In this chapter, the prophet presents five sets of questions and answers that reveal the superiority of God over everything we may think is powerful.

Question #1:

Who has measured the waters in the hollow of his hand, or with the breadth of his hand marked off the heavens? Who has held the dust of the earth in a basket, or weighed the mountains on the scales and the hills in a balance? Who has understood the Spirit of the Lord, or instructed Him as His counselor? Whom did the Lord consult to enlighten Him, and who taught Him the right way? Who was it that taught Him knowledge or showed Him the path of understanding? (Isaiah 40:12-14, NIV).

Answer #1:

Surely the nations are like a drop in a bucket; they are regarded as dust on the scales; He weighs the islands as though they were fine dust. Lebanon is not sufficient for altar fires, nor its animals enough for

burnt offerings. Before Him all the nations are as
nothing; they are regarded by Him as worthless and
less than nothing (Isaiah 40:15-17, *NIV*).

Conclusion:

God's power is far superior to even the strongest nations. In many countries of the world, the government attempts to provide for the needs of its citizens.
But we should not look to our government for provi-
sions and protection. God may use governments, but
we need to recognize that He is our source. He is our
defense. He is far superior.

****

Question #2:

To whom, then, will you compare God? What image
will you compare Him to? (Isaiah 40:18, *NIV*).

Answer #2:

As for an idol, a craftsman casts it, and a goldsmith
overlays it with gold and fashions silver chains for it.
A man too poor to present such an offering selects
wood that will not rot. He looks for a skilled craftsman to set up an idol that will not topple (Isaiah
40:19-20, *NIV*).

Conclusion:

God's power is far superior to idols. In Isaiah's day, the
people made idols of metal or wood, and then they
worshiped them. Our idols are also man-made, and
though we don't bow before them and utter prayers,
we worship them nonetheless. When I pursue pleasure, prestige, and possessions to meet my needs and
make me happy, it constitutes nothing less than idolatry. And just as the statues of silver and wood couldn't
satisfy, neither can these idols.

Question #3:

Do you not know? Have you not heard? Has it not been told you from the beginning? Have you not understood since the earth was founded? (Isaiah 40:21, *NIV*).

Answer #3:

He sits enthroned above the circle of the earth, and its people are like grasshoppers. He stretches out the heavens like a canopy, and spreads them out like a tent to live in. He brings princes to naught and reduces the rulers of this world to nothing. No sooner are they planted, no sooner are they sown, no sooner do they take root in the ground, than He blows on them and they wither, and a whirlwind sweeps them away like chaff (Isaiah 40:22, *NIV*).

Conclusion:

God's power is far superior to that of human leaders. The successes and failures of today's leaders are in plain view through television. We can see that our leaders are human and frail, yet we continue to count on them to solve our problems. We continue to believe that our difficulties would dissipate "if we could just elect so-and-so." God may choose to use a leader to help solve problems. But do we look to the infinite God or to sinful man for solutions?

Question #4:

"To whom will you compare Me? Or who is My equal?" says the Holy One (Isaiah 40:25, *NIV*).

Answer #4:

Lift up your eyes and look to the heavens: Who created all these? He who brings out the starry host one by one, and calls them each by name. Because of

His great power and mighty strength, not one of them
is missing (Isaiah 40:26, *NIV*).

<u>Conclusion:</u>

God is far superior to nature. Naturalists tell us there
is no God, that life has no meaning, yet *they* marvel at
"Mother Nature." God not only exists, He is also the
creator of such an immense universe that we measure
the distance between stars in light-years (the distance
traveled by light in one year: 186,000 miles/second x
60 seconds/minute x 60 minutes/hour x 24 hours/day
x 365 days/year). God the Creator is obviously far
superior to the creation itself. (I suggest a study of as-
tronomy to expand your view of the greatness of God,
but be careful to spit out the bones of naturalism.)

<u>Question #5:</u>

Why do you say, O Jacob, and complain, O Israel,
"My way is hidden from the Lord; my cause is disre-
garded by my God"? Do you not know? Have you not
heard? (Isaiah 40:27, 28, *NIV*).

<u>Answer #5:</u>

The Lord is the everlasting God, the Creator of the
ends of the earth. He will not grow tired or weary, and
His understanding no one can fathom. He gives
strength to the weary and increases the power of the
weak. Even youths grow tired and weary, and young
men stumble and fall; but those who hope in the Lord
will renew their strength. They will soar on wings like
eagles; they will run and not grow weary, they will
walk and not be faint (Isaiah 40:28-31, *NIV*).

<u>Conclusion:</u>

God is far superior to our problems. Why do I have
difficulty believing God in the midst of my problems?

Isn't it because I think He doesn't understand or doesn't care? The questions quoted in Isaiah are rebukes for unbelief. Surely people who had seen God work miracle after miracle, and whose prophets spoke the Word of God to them, should know more about the character of God! Surely they should know that God cares, God knows, and God gives strength. Surely I should know that, too.

When we depend on ourselves (verse 30), we inevitably get weary and stumble. This inevitably leads to frustration and ruin. We must wait on the Lord with the expectation that God will do what He wants to do in the way and the time He chooses.

Sometimes, I find myself saying, "I've tried everything. Now I guess I'll just trust the Lord," as if that's the last, hopeless gasp. Why does God become my last resort? His power and wisdom are far superior to the strongest and wisest people. Why is He not the One I instantly turn to at the faintest hint of need?

For centuries, men wrote and spoke of God in grand and majestic terms. He was called "The Almighty" most commonly. Today we are on more familiar terms with Him, and we think of Him as "Jesus, our Friend."

Years ago, people had a more accurate view of the power of God, but often lacked intimacy with Him. Today, we seek intimacy, but it is often at the expense of a grasp of His matchless power. We need to walk the tightrope between the two perspectives, clinging to a deep understanding of both His love and His power. As we become overwhelmed by both of these characteristics, we are compelled to love and serve Him. He alone is worthy of our love and obedience.

QUESTIONS

1. Does your concept of God match any of the misconceptions described? If so, which one? How has it affected you?

2. Is it easy or difficult to believe that God loves you? Why?

3. How would grasping the unfathomable love and awesome power of God affect your life (your goals, relationships, attitudes, and so forth)?

4. Read Revelation 4:8–5:14. List your observations of each song that is recorded. Does God seem worthy of your love and obedience? Why or why not?

Chapter 10
A Motivation for Our Choices: The Needs of People

The final days of Jesus' life on earth were filled with extremes. Many people had experienced His healing touch, His kindness, and His love, so they adored Him. The Pharisees saw Him as a threat to their authority, so they despised Him. The attitudes of most people toward Jesus were polarized; they either loved Him or hated Him.

As Jesus approached the end of His life, it would have been entirely normal for Him to be concerned with His reputation and His success. Yet even at the triumphal entry into Jerusalem—the height of His popularity—Jesus thought of others instead of Himself:

They . . . threw their cloaks on the colt and put Jesus on it. As He went along, people spread their cloaks on the road. When He came near the place where the road goes down the Mount of Olives, the whole crowd of disciples began joyfully to praise God in loud voices for all the miracles they had seen:

"Blessed is the King who comes in the name of the
Lord!" "Peace in heaven and glory in the highest!"
Some of the Pharisees in the crowd said to Jesus,
"Teacher, rebuke Your disciples!" "I tell you," He
replied, "if they keep quiet, the stones will cry out."
As He approached Jerusalem and saw the city, He
wept over it (Luke 19:35-41, *NIV*).

Jesus lived His life primarily for the glory of the Father,
but also because people desperately needed Him. Our desperate
needs haven't changed. Today they are even more obvious
because of television's ability to take us to the scene of calamity
after calamity in a moment's notice.

Looking beyond ourselves

Most of us are so absorbed in our own desires that we
seldom see that other people have needs. We are more interested in getting a little more comfortable than in relieving the
pain of others. We are so busy making a little more money,
learning a little more, having a little nicer party, or fine-tuning
our tennis topspin a little more that we are oblivious to the
needs of other people.

Yet when we realize that our desperate needs for security
and purpose have been completely met through Jesus' unconditional love, we can turn our attention outward, to the staggering needs of others. The Christian life should be full of joy, but
Jesus' life was also full of compassion. "Jesus wept" is not only
the shortest verse in the Bible, but also an expression of the
empathy of Christ for those in need. His compassion compelled
Him to act relentlessly and tirelessly to help others.

I remember riding a bus through the streets of New
Delhi. It was a heart-wrenching experience. Eight million
people in the city reflected the widespread symptoms of hunger,
loneliness, and despair. Only a handful of Christians lived there
to shine as lights in that idolatrous Hindu culture.

I made a video of my trip to India and Thailand. The quality of the video was poor, yet those who have seen it have been profoundly affected. The vivid pictures and interviews cut through the layers of Western insulation. One young man came to me with tears in his eyes after he saw the video and said, "Tonight I decided to go into pioneer missions." Today that young man is preparing to go to Argentina.

We can become so caught up in our own worlds that we become quite calloused to the pain others experience. Let's examine several areas that will remind us of these needs.

Worldwide needs

At this writing, some twenty-one wars and civil wars are going on in the world. When we see the news on TV or read the paper, we need to remember that these conflicts are more than news items. Fathers and sons (and too often women and children) are being killed. Families are being torn apart. Intense hatred and oppression spreads. Fear is ever present.

The rise of terrorism in recent years is another horror to civilized people. It has been estimated that terrorist activity has escalated from ten incidents per month in 1970 to ten per day in 1985—a 3000% increase! And again, each of these events is not just a statistic. It represents the excruciating pain of senseless injury and death. Fear, hatred, and hopelessness are very real consequences of this heinous crime.

Abortion is taking the lives of more and more unborn children. Sanctioned by political bodies from the United Nations to national and state governments, abortion is considered a viable means of birth control. Since the 1963 Supreme Court decision (Roe vs. Wade), millions of abortions have been performed in the United States—which is only a fraction of the global number.

Consider that in World War II, all of the industrial and military might of the major nations of the world was committed to killing people. Including the seven million Jews murdered by Hitler in the Holocaust and the famine in the Hunan Province of China, combat and noncombat deaths during the war amounted to about 55 million people—roughly the same number of unborn children aborted each year throughout the world today.

Famine is another major world concern. The one in Ethiopia has been brought to international awareness recently, yet hunger is not restricted to one portion of Africa. The United Nations estimates that 40,000 children die of starvation and related diseases *every day*. This is a startling statistic that includes only a part of the world's population.

Other desperate needs around the world and in America include the plight of the poor, the homeless, the sick, the handicapped, the aged, and many others who live in abject need. Yet so many of us are absorbed in the pursuit of pleasure, oblivious to those around us who desperately need help.

Here and now

We may see wars and famines on the evening news, shake our heads, and think disconsolately, "How can I do anything about that?" But the needs of people next door or in our own homes are often just as real—and far more accessible.

The divorce rate has reached 50% in America, and the effects of losing a secure family base cannot be overestimated. In some segments of our society, up to 80% of homes are without a resident father. In many others, the father is far more concerned about his own pleasure and success than the needs of his family. Surely the preponderance of drugs, alcohol, and sexual activity among young people is a reflection of this problem.

Recently I have noted the striking contrast between college students who have stable, loving parents and those who are from divorced homes (or homes where the parents failed to communicate love and acceptance). Those from stable homes are much more comfortable meeting new people, and trying new responsibilities. The ones from unstable backgrounds tended toward extremes of behavior: either withdrawal to avoid the anticipated pain of rejection, or overcompensated behavior to call attention to themselves.

Another symptom of personal needs is hopelessness. I'm not referring here to a lack of goals. Many people do have goals: a big house, a new car, a nice spouse, perfect children, long vacations, a good-paying job, and so forth. They anticipate that such things will provide true happiness. But these goals, if and when achieved, simply do not satisfy. So the people set their sights on a bigger house, a newer car, longer vacations, a higher paying job, and a better spouse, only to find they are still restless and unfulfilled. This realization leads to hopelessness.

The struggle to acquire more and more numbs people to the things of true value—deep relationships with Christ (and others), and the life purpose of honoring Jesus. Even when they realize that vain pursuits will never satisfy, they keep trying harder, but with less hope. We need to befriend these people so we can represent Jesus Christ to them. As Henry David Thoreau wrote, "Most men live lives of quiet desperation."

Perhaps the most desperate and poignant pain in human existence is guilt. People try all manner of means to lessen the pain of knowing they have done or are doing wrong. They deny it, they justify it, and the few who admit it try to do enough good things to make up for it, but it is never enough.

Psychologists Bruce Narramore and Bill Counts see the painful effects of guilt with clarity and perception. They write:

In almost every area of our lives we confront the damage done by guilt. Guilt has a way of binding us down, or pressuring us, and of robbing us of freedom and spontaneity. And none of us is entirely free of guilt's influence. The perfectionist housewife; the worrier; the aggressive, driven businessman; the insomniac; the straight "A" student; and the searching religious person are all partially motivated by hidden guilt. Each is trying something to develop a sense of self-acceptance or inner harmony. Must we live as slaves to guilt and its various disguises?

Eternal needs

The personal needs just described are quite evident to most people because the pain is experienced here and now. Eternal needs are not so evident.

Heaven is fun to think about. Hell is not. Some theologians question whether hell is indeed a reality. They profess the doctrine of *universalism* which says that a loving God wouldn't send anyone to hell. All, then, will be saved. It sounds nice and convenient (especially for those who reject Christ), but it flies in the face of the irrefutable teaching of God's Word.

Let's look at what the Scriptures actually say about God's judgment, hell, and the eternal consequences of sin:

If we deliberately keep on sinning after we have received the knowledge of the truth, no sacrifice for sins is left, but only a fearful expectation of judgment and of raging fire that will consume the enemies of God. Anyone who rejected the law of Moses died without mercy on the testimony of two or three witnesses. How much more severely do you think a man deserves to be punished who has trampled the Son of God under foot, who has treated as an unholy thing the blood of the covenant that sanctified him, and who has insulted the Spirit of grace? For we know Him who said, "It is Mine to avenge; I will repay," and again, "The Lord will judge His people." It is a dreadful thing to fall into the hands of the living God" (Hebrews 10:26-31, *NIV*).

If your eye causes you to sin, pluck it out. It is
better for you to enter the kingdom of God with one
eye than to have two eyes and be thrown into hell,
where "their worm does not die, and the fire is not
quenched." Everyone will be salted with fire (Mark
9:47, 48, *NIV*).

He left the crowd and went into the house. His
disciples came to Him and said, "Explain to us the
parable of the weeds in the field." He answered, "The
one who sowed the good seed is the Son of Man. The
field is the world, and the good seed stands for the
sons of the kingdom. The weeds are the sons of the
evil one, and the enemy who sows them is the devil.
The harvest is the end of the age, and the harvesters
are angels. As the weeds are pulled up and burned in
the fire, so it will be at the end of the age. The Son of
Man will send out His angels, and they will weed out
of His kingdom everything that causes sin and all who
do evil. They will throw them into the fiery furnace,
where there will be weeping and gnashing of teeth.
Then the righteous will shine like the sun in the
kingdom of their Father. He who has ears, let him
hear" (Matthew 13:36-43, *NIV*).

All your pomp has been brought down to the
grave, along with the noise of your harps; maggots
are spread out beneath you and worms cover you
(Isaiah 14:11, *NIV*).

I saw a great white throne and Him who was seated
on it. Earth and sky fled from His presence, and there
was no place for them. And I saw the dead, great and
small, standing before the throne, and books were

opened. Another book was opened, which is the book
of life. The dead were judged according to what they
had done as recorded in the books. The sea gave up
the dead that were in it, and death and Hades gave up
the dead that were in them, and each person was
judged according to what he had done. Then death
and Hades were thrown into the lake of fire. The lake
of fire is the second death. If anyone's name was not
found written in the book of life, he was thrown into
the lake of fire (Revelation 20:11-15, *NIV*).

These are not pleasant passages, but they are God's Word
and they speak the truth about eternal condemnation for those
apart from Christ.

When we see people who are self-righteous, drunk, or
perverted in some way, do we turn away in disgust? Or do we
see them as "distressed and downtrodden, like sheep without a
shepherd"? Do we realize that it is only by the grace of God
that we are not in the same state? We would do well to remember Paul's words to the self-righteous Corinthian church:

Do you not know that the unrighteous shall not
inherit the kingdom of God? Do not be deceived;
neither fornicators, nor idolaters, nor adulterers, nor
effeminate, nor homosexuals, nor thieves, nor the
covetous, nor drunkards, nor revilers, nor swindlers,
shall inherit the kingdom of God. And such were
some of you; but you were washed, but you were
sanctified, but you were justified in the name of the
Lord Jesus Christ, and in the Spirit of our God
(I Corinthians 6:9-11).

Choosing to be available: Example #1

The great English pastor, Charles Spurgeon, had a clear
perception of the eternal destiny of men and women. In 1854,

a cholera epidemic swept across Great Britain. Thousands were dying. At one point, two people known by Spurgeon were approaching the same fate with far different perspectives. Spurgeon first went to see a man who was dying:

I stood by his side, and spoke to him, but he gave me no answer. I spoke again, but the only consciousness he had was a foreboding of terror, mingled with the stupor of approaching death. Soon, even that was gone, for sense had fled, and I stood there, a few minutes, sighing with the poor woman who had watched over him, and altogether hopeless about his soul. Gazing at his face, I perceived that he was dead, and that his soul had departed.

That man, in his lifetime, had been wont to jeer at me. In strong language, he had often denounced me as a hypocrite. Yet he was no sooner smitten by the darts of death than he sought my presence and counsel, no doubt feeling in his heart that I was a servant of God, though he did not care to own it with his lips. There I stood, unable to help him. Promptly as I had responded to his call, what could I do but look at his corpse, and mourn over a lost soul? He had, when in health, wickedly refused Christ, yet in his death agony he had superstitiously sent for me. Too late, he sighed for the ministry of reconciliation, and sought to enter in at the closed door, but he was not able. There was no space left him then for repentance, for he had wasted the opportunities which God had long granted to him.

In contrast to his experience with the unbelieving man, Spurgeon continued, describing a woman he knew:

I went home, and was soon called away again; that time, to see a young woman. She also was in the last extremity, but it was a fair, fair sight. She was sing-

ing—though she knew she was dying—and talking to
those round about her, telling her brothers and sisters
to follow her to heaven, bidding good-bye to her
father, and all the while smiling as if it had been her
marriage day. She was happy and blessed. I never saw
more conspicuously in my life, than I did that morning, the difference there is between one who feareth
God and one who feareth Him not (C. H. Spurgeon,
Autobiography, Volume I: The Early Years, The Banner
of Truth Trust).

It has been said that we shouldn't talk about hell to anyone unless we have tears in our eyes. That is true enough, but
the absence of tears is not an excuse to overlook the reality of
hell. Instead, the statement should serve as a reminder of the
gravity of the issue: people who reject Christ will experience
the righteous wrath of Almighty God for all eternity.

If that thought doesn't move us to tell others about the
Gospel, maybe we need to reflect on the devastation from
which Christ has rescued us. It should be a responsibility and
privilege to talk to people about their eternal destiny.

Choosing to be available: Example #2

The need for each person to hear the Gospel is immense.
Consider the number of people in the world who have never
heard the Gospel. Robertson McQuilkin, president of Columbia Bible College and Columbia Graduate School of Bible and
Missions, estimates that, "three of four people have never heard
with understanding the way to life in Christ and, even more
tragic, half the people of the world cannot hear because there is
no one near enough to tell them."

Many of us spend our lives trying to avoid acknowledging the needs of other people. We seek the shelter and comfort
of Christian fellowship, splitting theological hairs with only an
occasional foray into the real world. We blatantly seek earthly

goals of business success, social status, and pleasure, showing little concern for the eternal needs of those around us. We believe that people will think we are weird if we talk to them about Christ.

Yet a few are willing to help meet the needs of others. Nathan, a student at the University of Texas, raised the money to go on a summer missions trip to Africa last year. There were easier ways to spend the summer, but he determined to make himself available to be used by the Lord!

One Sunday Nathan was asked to speak at a church in one of the central African countries where his team was traveling. As he spoke of the grace of God, he noticed that the pastor looked quite disturbed. When Nathan finished, the pastor took him to another room and said, "I have never heard what you have told us today. Please tell me more."

While the service continued, Nathan led the pastor to a personal relationship with Christ. Then the pastor went out to speak to the people, and he led almost the entire congregation to the same type of relationship.

Choosing to be available: Example #3

If we are available to God, He will lead us to situations where He can use us. Yet we must realize that these areas of ministry are seldom easy, lest we become discouraged. The story of Roland Bingham is one of the most powerful stories in the history of the church, and should encourage anyone who may be reluctant to "hang in there."

In the late 19th century, Walter Gowans studied missions in his native Canada. He became so gripped by the need for the Gospel in Africa's interior, he felt led by God to go there. Even though there were 60 million Africans and not a single missionary in that disease-infested area, Gowans had difficulty finding sponsors. The mission societies were aware of the dangers in the interior of Africa, known at that time as the

Sudan, and believed it was useless to send missionaries there.
So Gowans sailed for England to find support.

Undoubtedly, Gowans's most zealous supporter was his
mother, who tried to recruit others to go to the Sudan with her
son. Mrs. Gowans heard Roland Bingham speak at a church,
and invited him to her home. She was impressed with Bingham
and ardently urged him to join her son. Bingham wrote:

The next morning, when I went to call on Mrs.
Gowans, it was to announce that I expected to sail in
two weeks to join her son in a common enterprise.
Was she glad? She was the whole board and I was
accepted on the spot.

Bingham went to New York where he asked Thomas
Kent, a friend of Walter Gowans, to join the expedition. The
two men sailed in the spring of 1893 to join Gowans and travel
on to Africa. When the three arrived in Lagos, they were told
by other missionaries that they had no chance of survival in
the interior. The head of the Methodist Missions said, "Young
men, you will never see the Sudan; your children will never see
the Sudan; your grandchildren may."

But the absence of missionaries in the Sudan was precisely why they had come. They had determined to go on when
Bingham became sick. They decided that he should stay in
Lagos and set up a supply base. But in less than a year both
Gowans and Kent were dead. Gowans contracted dysentery,
was captured by a slave-raiding chieftain, and died shortly after
his release. Kent died of malaria.

Bingham returned to New York, enrolled in a Bible
school and pastored a small church. He was devastated by the
deaths of his companions. He reflected:

My faith was being shaken to the very foundation.
Why should those most anxious to carry out the
Lord's commands and to give His Gospel to millions
in darkness be cut off right at the beginning of their

career? Many questions faced me—Was the Bible
merely an evolution of human thought, even biased
thought, or was it a divine revelation? For months the
struggle over this great issue went on before I was
finally brought back to the solid rock.

The desperate needs in the Sudan continued to disturb
Bingham. So seven years after his first try, with renewed faith,
Bingham led two other men back to Africa. Again, he became
ill. The other two men promised to go ahead, but when they
heard the ominous warnings of the missionaries in Lagos, they
quickly sailed back home. Bingham was deeply depressed:

It would have been easier for me, perhaps, had I
died in Africa, for on the homeward journey I died
another death. Everything seemed to have failed, and
when while I was gradually regaining strength in
Britain, a fateful cable reached me with word that my
two companions were arriving shortly, I went through
the darkest period of my whole life.

But Bingham refused to give up. He returned to Canada
and recruited volunteers to join him for a third attempt in
1901. Paddling 500 miles up the Niger River, the scene was
much like the old "Tarzan" movies. This time, he was successful
in establishing a mission station at Patigi.

But again, tragedy struck. Within two years, only one of
the team remained. One died and two had to be sent home due
to severe illness. Bingham held on by a toehold.

Slowly, others joined Bingham in the Sudan, and the
tiny mission station was replicated in other remote areas. In
1928, Bingham's Sudan Interior Mission began its work in
southern Ethiopia, but the early years saw little fruitfulness.

By 1935, when the Italian army invaded Ethiopia, there
were only seventeen Ethiopian Christians. The British and
American embassies advised the missionaries of the SIM to
evacuate, but they decided to stay. When the missionaries were

forced to evacuate two years later, the number of converts had
grown to forty-eight. The missionaries were sad as they drove
away from the mission station:

> As we turned the last corner around the mountain
> and saw in the distance the wave of their hands in
> farewell, we wondered what would happen to the
> little flickering flame of Gospel light that had been lit
> in the midst of so much darkness. Would these young
> Christians, with no more of the Word of God in their
> own language than the Gospel of Mark and a few
> small booklets of selected Scripture portions to guide
> and teach them, be able to stand under the
> persecution that would inevitably come?

The Italians severely persecuted the little flock. The
leaders received 100 lashes; one was given 400 lashes; three of
them died. But under the cruelty, the church grew.

In 1941, the British drove the Italians out of Ethiopia.
When the SIM missionaries returned, they suspected that their
little flock would have dwindled. They could hardly believe
what they found. The band of forty-eight believers had miraculously grown to 10,000. There were almost 100 congregations.

The thrill of the news overwhelmed Roland Bingham. In
the excitement, as he made plans to go to Ethiopia to see the
mighty work of God, he died of a heart attack.

When we look at the miracle of the Ethiopian church's
explosive growth under Italian persecution, it is easy to forget
those early years of heartbreak and death. Yet the glories of
1941 would not have happened without Bingham's tenacious
faith from the turn of the century until that time.

After the first and second attempts to enter the Sudan,
undoubtedly people said, "You've done all you could do. It's
obviously not God's will for missionaries to go into the Sudan."
Others probably were less diplomatic and told Bingham,
"You're crazy!" But Roland Bingham answered to a higher

authority than the ideas of people or the comforts of Western civilization. He kept going.

When the apostle Paul was in prison, he wrote a letter to the church at Philippi. He wanted to send someone to help and encourage them, but virtually everyone had deserted him. However, there was one person he could count on:

I hope in the Lord Jesus to send Timothy to you shortly, so that I also may be encouraged when I learn of your condition. For I have no one else of kindred spirit who will genuinely be concerned for your welfare. For they all seek after their own interests, not those of Christ Jesus. But you know of his proven worth that he served with me in the furtherance of the gospel like a child serving his father (Philippians 2:19-22).

I have to ask myself, "If Paul were alive today, would he send me, or would he consider me to be seeking after my own interests?" Would he send you?

QUESTIONS

1. *Why are most of us so oblivious to the needs of others?*

2. *What has helped you stay in touch with others' needs?*

3. *Which need described in this chapter grips you most? Why?*

4. *What are some specific steps you can take to help meet this need?*

5. *Read Matthew 25:31-46. What are some ways you can apply this passage? Be specific.*

6. *What are the similarities and differences between being guilt motivated and being grace motivated?*

Chapter 11

We Reap What We Choose to Sow

Peter was very bright, as he proved by making almost 1400 on his SAT, but he didn't like to study. Anytime somebody in the dorm wanted to play cards, Peter was ready to play. Anybody want to play basketball? Peter was always ready to go. And parties? Peter could find them every night of the week.

He made a 1.7 GPA in each of his first two terms, and he was put on probation. I saw him at the beginning of the next term and he lamented his situation. "I'm really going to have to do better this time," Peter said with conviction. But less than a week later, I saw him wearing sweats and carrying cleats at a baseball game. He told me, "I think I can make the varsity if I can control my curveball."

The weeks passed and I didn't see Peter. After finals I saw him at the mall in our hometown. After we talked about his inability to throw his curve for strikes, I asked him, "Well, how did you do last term?"

"I pulled a 4," Peter said with a hint of a grin.

I was shocked. "Really! That's great!"

The grin broadened, "Well, it's not too great. I pulled a 0.4." He laughed at his joke. "I won't be going back, I guess."

Peter had reaped what he had sown. Not more. Not less.

Sow what?

An irrefutable consequence of life is the principle of sowing and reaping. This principle is misunderstood and misused by many today. But taken in proper perspective, it gives us another compelling reason to choose to live for Christ. Paul wrote to the Galatian believers:

> Do not be deceived: God cannot be mocked. A man reaps what he sows. The one who sows to please his sinful nature, from that nature will reap destruction; the one who sows to please the Spirit, from the Spirit will reap eternal life. Let us not become weary in doing good, for at the proper time we will reap a harvest if we do not give up. Therefore, as we have opportunity, let us do good to all people, especially to those who belong to the family of believers (Galatians 6:7-10, NIV).

This principle applies in virtually every area of life. When a farmer plants corn, he harvests corn, not beans. When a person is kind to others, people are generally kind to him. When a farmer neglects feeding his cattle, they become sick and die. And when a person is bitter and sarcastic toward others, they tend to be that way toward him. It is a principle of nature, of relationships, and of the spiritual realm.

When I was in high school, I was voted "Wittiest in the Class." You could spell my kind of wit: S-A-R-C-A-S-M. Slicing people to pieces like a rapier was a normal part of my life. To someone with oversized ears, I might say, "Hey, Fred, how'd you get those dishes glued to the side of your head?" No one was exempt: classmates, teachers, coaches, teams, anybody, and everybody. It was fun to come up with the most biting line at a particular instance. I got a lot of laughs.

It was fun, that is, as long as I was the one being funny at the expense of others' feelings. It was not so funny when I was on the *receiving* end. And the strange thing was, the more I cut others down, the more they cut me down in return. Soon the fun turned into a war, and the war was very painful to me. It was time to tone down the "wit."

I still have a penchant for sarcasm, and I still get hurt when others respond with sarcastic remarks toward me. I realize more and more that I am simply reaping what I have sowed.

"Isn't it selfish to expect to reap?"

I've been asked, "Isn't it selfish to be motivated by the law of sowing and reaping?" I don't believe the issue is selfishness vs. unselfishness, but rather wisdom vs. foolishness. It is prudent to make choices in which we will reap benefits for ourselves and honor for Christ. Only a fool would knowingly harm himself and dishonor the Lord.

A good friend of mine is a dentist in Missouri. Wes is well educated, athletic, and gifted in many areas. He had to choose how to spend his time and energy. One option was to take new clients and make as much money as possible. Another was to spend his time playing sports "with the guys." But instead, he chose to spend his time with the Lord, with his family, and in ministry. He works hard, but making money is not his top priority. He is now reaping the results of these values in his own spiritual maturity, a happy, stable family, and profound effects on people in his community.

The opposite situation is all too evident. Many people have abandoned quality family time and ministry in order to feed their insatiable desires for pleasure and success. The consequences they reap are devastating: guilt, shallow relationships, hopelessness, and bitterness, to name a few.

The choice is mine—and yours. We must not be deceived about the consequences of our choices.

"What will I reap?"

Another question people ask is, "What will I reap?" Prosperity theology, so prevalent today, tells us that we will reap health, wealth, and happiness. If we don't, our faith just isn't strong enough. Such theology comes from a selective reading of the Bible. While there are passages that promise blessings, there are no promises of continual, pervasive blessings in every area of our lives.

Paul wrote to Timothy, "All who desire to live godly in Christ Jesus will be persecuted" (II Timothy 3:12). And Jesus told His disciples:

If the world hates you, keep in mind that it hated Me first. If you belonged to the world, it would love you as its own. As it is, you do not belong to the world, but I have chosen you out of the world. That is why the world hates you. Remember the words I spoke to you: "No servant is greater than his master." If they persecuted Me, they will persecute you also. If they obeyed My teaching, they will obey yours also. They will treat you this way because of My name, for they do not know the One who sent Me" (John 15:18-21, NIV).

And in another instance, Jesus clarified His mission so His followers would know what to expect:

Do not suppose that I have come to bring peace to the earth. I did not come to bring peace, but a sword. For I have come to turn "a man against his father, a daughter against her mother, a daughter-in-law against her mother-in-law—a man's enemies will be the members of his own household." Anyone who loves his father or mother more than Me is not

worthy of Me; anyone who loves his son or daughter
more than Me is not worthy of Me; and anyone who
does not take his cross and follow Me is not worthy of
Me. Whoever finds his life will lose it, and whoever
loses his life for My sake will find it" (Matthew 10:34-
39, NIV).

These passages are not popular texts among the health,
wealth, and happiness preachers. If we truly live for Christ, we
will reap both the joy of knowing Him as well as the rejection
He Himself endured. That's a promise!

"When will I reap?"

A third question is, "When will I reap?" Again, prosperity theologians would tell us that we will receive immediate
benefits, but the Scriptures indicate otherwise:

Let us not become weary in doing good, for at the
proper time we will reap a harvest if we do not give up
(Galatians 6:9, NIV).

When is the proper time? Who knows? God's record
keeping system is undeniably fair and just, yet is not easily
understood by our limited insight. Some people seem to receive
a lot of rewards without much delay. For others, a much longer
period ensues between good actions and God's reward. Still
others will not be rewarded until the Lord returns. "When the
Chief Shepherd appears, you will receive the unfading crown of
glory" (I Peter 5:4). Whether now or later, the principle stands:
We will reap what we sow.

Both prosperity theology and our instant-oriented society advocate that we should have life easy, and it should be easy
right now. People have difficulty with the perspective that they
may have to wait to receive something. A farmer understands
that he can't plant seeds and expect a bumper crop the next
day—or the next week—or the next month. It takes an entire
growing season until the harvest comes, and in between the

planting and the harvesting is a lot of hard work. It is certain that we will reap what we sow, but the "sowing" may not come as quickly as we would like.

Ultimately, we will reap what we have sown when we stand before Christ to give an account of our lives (I Corinthians 3:11-15). All who have trusted in Jesus as Savior will experience thankfulness to have escaped eternal condemnation and to have entered into the very presence of Christ. The measure of joy, however, will vary for each person according to the choices which were made for Jesus' honor. For some, joy will be tempered by the heap of ashes that represents self-centeredness. Others will hear those words that will be reward enough in themselves: "Well done, good and faithful servant."

That day will come. We have opportunities every day to choose love, honor, and conquest over selfishness and pride. The results of our choices will be evident on that day!

"Oops! What if I've made some bad choices?"

But what if we've made some bad choices? God forgives, refreshes, and provides new opportunities. Do mistakes place us out of God's will forever? No! We need not be slaves to indecision and fear. God is a God of freedom and grace. As you seek to grow spiritually, you will make mistakes. Don't give up. Keep responding to His love and power by obeying and loving Him.

The true story of two brothers illustrates the options we have. Robert is a mortgage broker in New York City. Craig is unemployed, living in Oklahoma. Though brothers, their stories are as different as night and day.

Robert is a Christian who has determined to honor the Lord in every way he can. He is successful, but business success doesn't consume him. His family is a model for the neighborhood. When people have problems, they come to see Robert and his wife Sharon. Their children know they are loved, and are stable and secure (with a normal share of mischief).

God uses Robert and Sharon in many ways: counseling, comforting, sharing Christ, giving to the church, and leading Bible study groups. Like all families, times aren't always rosy. Robert's business often puts him under a lot of pressure, but fellow workers can count on him to be calm and stable. His faith in Christ is evident, but not overpowering, and people know he has answers to their problems.

Such stability is entirely absent from Craig's life. He may be a Christian (no one, including Craig, seems to be sure). His life lacks purpose and direction. At 37, he is always looking for that elusive "big deal to close."

After being married twice, Craig is single again. He recently expressed interest in a wealthy divorcée. He told his parents, "Then I could have all I want and I'd be happy."

Craig spends so much money partying that he could fund most of the national debt. He has a lot of "friends" who enjoy his parties. He drinks a lot, and Robert suspects that he may be getting into drugs. In spite of all the good times and fast cars, there is one word that characterizes Craig's life: miserable.

The one thing Robert and Craig have in common is that they are reaping the consequences of the values and life-styles they have chosen.

Last year I met a college student, Carl, who said he was a Christian. A quick glance around his room made me question his statement. Pinups plastered the walls and whiskey bottles were stacked as trophies in the window. As we talked, I realized that Carl was not aware of the consequences of his recently acquired life-style. I told him about Robert and Craig, and then I read the Galatians 6 passage about sowing and reaping.

I was very concerned about this young man who was on the verge of establishing a destructive life-style. Thankfully, Carl realized something was wrong. As I finished telling the stories and reading the Scripture, I noticed his eyes had filled with tears.

During the next several weeks, Carl became acquainted with a group of students who were serious about their faith in Christ. His life began to change. The Spirit of God began transforming his values, relationships, and habits. The pinups and bottles went in the dumpster the first week. Carl found real joy and fulfillment in his renewed relationship with Christ and his new relationships with other Christians.

Why are so many of us unaware of the results of ungodly life-styles? We need to take notice when we see people like Craig. The sobering consequences of bad decisions can point us to Christ.

We have considered some compelling motivations to choose to live for Christ. For one thing, Jesus is worthy of our love and obedience. For another, people have desperate needs. The obvious conclusion is that it is foolish to live for ourselves:

> Christ's love compels us, because we are convinced
> that one died for all, and therefore all died. And He
> died for all, that those who live should no longer live
> for themselves but for Him who died for them and
> was raised again (II Corinthians 5:14, 15, *NIV*).

Everyone comes to the same crossroads. You can live for yourself. Or you can live for Christ. But give this matter serious thought because you will surely reap what you sow. The choice is yours.

QUESTIONS

1. *What are the logical consequences of your current attitudes, values, and life-style?*

2. *Read Galatians 6:7-10. Does the fact that you will reap the consequences of your life-style encourage you or frighten you? Why? What do you need to change?*

Chapter 12
Choosing Security

Dr. Lawrence Crabb has written that God created man with two fundamental needs: *security* and *significance*. He defines security as "a convinced awareness of being unconditionally and totally loved without needing to change in order to win love; loved by a love which is freely given, which cannot be earned and therefore cannot be lost." Significance is "a realization of personal adequacy for a job truly important, a job whose results will not evaporate with time ... a job which fundamentally involves having a meaningful impact on another person" (*The Institute of Biblical Counseling Training Manual*).

The drive to obtain security and significance is a built-in instinct based on a God-given need. But there is a catch. God has created us so that only He can meet that need. Isaiah quoted the Lord:

Every one who thirsts, come to the waters; and you who have no money come, buy and eat. Come, buy wine and milk without money and without cost. Why

do you spend money for what is not bread, and your
wages for what does not satisfy? Listen carefully to
Me, and eat what is good, and delight yourself in
abundance (Isaiah 55:1, 2).

Our own resources will not quench our thirst for security
and significance. That thirst can only be completely satisfied by
God. In a parallel to the Isaiah passage, Christ proclaimed to
multitudes of people:

If any man is thirsty, let him come to Me and drink.
He who believes in Me, as the Scripture said, "From
His innermost being shall flow rivers of living water"
(John 7:37, 38).

Jesus plainly declared that He alone could provide genuine and lasting peace, fulfillment, and purpose. Yet as we have
seen, Satan has counterfeited the security and significance that
only Christ can give, attempting to keep us from worshiping
the One who deserves honor, praise, and obedience.

Robert McGee has written of mankind's predicament:
"Separated from God and His Word, people have only their
abilities and the opinions of others on which to base their
worth, and the circumstances around them will ultimately
control the way they feel about themselves" (*The Search for
Significance*, Rapha Publishing). But our performance and the
fickle approval of others are very poor substitutes for the
unconditional love and compelling purposes of God.

Performance and acceptance

Acceptance or rejection by other people is almost always
based on our ability to perform. When I was in college, one
summer I worked as a laborer for a big construction company.
My boss was a foreman named Shorty. It was Shorty's first time
as a foreman, and he didn't quite know what to do with the
laborers during lulls in the construction schedule. One day he
told several of us, "I want each of you to dig a hole right here."

Here? I thought. *We aren't putting a wall here. There's no need for a hole.* I said to Shorty, "OK, what do you want us to do after we've dug them?"

"Fill 'em back up," Shorty mumbled as he walked away.

We looked at each other, feeling ridiculous and humiliated. "No way!" I said. Shorty turned around and walked toward me. "Do you refuse to do like I told you?" he snarled.

I tried to explain that we could find more profitable ways to spend our time, but Shorty was beyond listening to reason. (Perhaps I could have been a bit more diplomatic!) He glared at me and said, "You're fired! Get out of here!"

But at that moment Shorty's supervisor, Bill, drove up. It just so happened that Bill had been my football coach. He had been an all SEC center at the University of Georgia. I, in turn, was an all-star center for Bill's team. So he liked me a lot.

Shorty knew nothing of my history with Bill as he told him of my insolence and why he had just fired me. He was shocked when Bill asked for my side of the story. I told Bill exactly what had happened. Bill looked at me and said, "Pick up your shovel and go find something constructive to do, Pat." Shorty's jaw dropped. Bill had rehired me!

The air was tense the next day. Shorty was looking for an excuse to fire me. Sure enough, late in the morning, he told me that I hadn't done something right. With deep satisfaction, he growled, "You're fired!" But Shorty didn't know that Bill had driven up a few minutes earlier had seen our confrontation. He took Shorty aside, and motioned for me to keep working.

Now Shorty was steaming! He waited to pounce on me like a hungry leopard watching a gazelle. A couple of days later he announced that I'd taken too long on a break. With a blend of joy and vengeance, he said for the third time, "You're fired!"

I got into my car and began to drive off, but then I saw a company car. Could it be Bill? Yes! He asked why I was leaving, and I told him what had happened. "Come with me," he said.

I followed him back to the construction site. You should have seen Shorty's face! Bill and Shorty had a chat, and I was rehired for the third time! After that, Shorty seldom spoke to me. I just did whatever he told the other laborers to do.

My relationships with Shorty and Bill may seem like a classic contrast of rejection and unconditional acceptance, but they aren't. Shorty's response was obviously rejection. Bill's response seemed like acceptance, but like Shorty's, it was based squarely on my performance.

True, if I hadn't been the all-star center on Bill's team, I doubt that I would have received preferential treatment. After all, other laborers certainly weren't treated that way. And I doubt if Bill would have rehired me—three times—to the great embarrassment of one of his foremen. But even though I enjoyed Bill's acceptance, I knew I was expected to perform well to deserve it. It was not unconditional acceptance. Such a no-strings-attached acceptance is a rare commodity in our world.

Misperceptions destroy security

Any kind of acceptance feels better than rejection. The driving need for love, security, and purpose compels us to look for satisfaction anywhere we can find it. If we believe success, approval, comfort, or beauty will meet our needs, then we will pursue those things with a passion and intensity that amounts to worship. All people, Christian or non-Christian, worship whatever they believe will meet their deepest personal needs.

A growing number of us have experienced parental neglect or come from families with compulsive disorders—alcoholism, drug abuse, workaholism, eating disorders, or physical or emotional abuse. Almost inevitably, people from these families try to ease the growing pain of rejection by trying to please people. They are, in fact, driven to please people out of the pain of guilt, the fear of condemnation, and the faint hope that they can be loved and accepted.

Guilt and fear are powerful motivators, but cruel task-masters. And anytime someone writes about obedience, there is the risk of prodding a guilt-motivated person into more self-condemnation and fear of rejection. But if your response to God (and others) is based these emotions, you need to begin to be honest with God (and with a close friend) about your feelings. Spend time reflecting on the love and grace of God.

Self-effort and condemnation are commonly traveled roads, but there is a better way. By the Word of God energized by the Spirit of God, we have the privilege to "declare the praises of Him who called you out of darkness into His wonderful light" (I Peter 2:9, NIV). That is a far different motivation, which results in far different effects on us and on others.

To counteract the overwhelming abundance of messages from friends, families, and the media about the importance of pleasing others, it is crucial that we develop a deep conviction about Christ's ability to meet our deepest needs. How does He meet our needs for security and significance? There are many doctrines we could examine to answer this question, but three are sufficient to build a strong spiritual and emotional base: *propitiation*, *justification*, and *reconciliation*.

These doctrines are not obscure or esoteric. They are bedrocks of faith, yet their implications are often bypassed. They clearly communicate that our security is founded on the unconditional love, forgiveness, and acceptance of God.

Security factor #1: Propitiation

The biblical truth of propitiation tells us we are deeply loved by God. John wrote:

This is how God showed his love among us: He sent his one and only Son into the world that we might live through Him. This is love: not that we loved God, but that He loved us and sent His Son as an atoning sacrifice for our sins (I John 4:9, 10, NIV).

The word "propitiate" means to satisfy God's righteous wrath against sin. *But wait,* you may be thinking, *I thought we were talking about God's love. What's this about God's wrath?*

When a jeweler wants to show off a diamond, what does he use? Usually, he selects something dark and dull, like black velvet, so the brilliance of the diamond can be seen more clearly. Similarly, in order to understand the magnitude of the love of God, we need to see it in the context of His wrath.

God's wrath is His righteous vengeance against sin. His wrath is totally justified. It is a response of His holiness in regard to our desire to steal glory from Him. In his New Testament letters, Paul made it clear that, because of sin, we deserve death (Romans 6:23). In a graphic depiction of an event that will shock the world on some future day, Paul described the terrible retribution that people will receive because of sin:

> God is just: He will pay back trouble to those who
> trouble you and give relief to you who are troubled,
> and to us as well. This will happen when the Lord
> Jesus is revealed from heaven in blazing fire with His
> powerful angels. He will punish those who do not
> know God and do not obey the gospel of our Lord
> Jesus. They will be punished with everlasting destruc-
> tion and shut out from the presence of the Lord and
> from the majesty of His power on the day He comes
> to be glorified in His holy people and to be marveled
> at among all those who have believed. This includes
> you, because you believed our testimony to you"
> (II Thessalonians 1:6-10, *NIV*).

We deserve punishment, but Christ has become our substitute. He satisfied the righteous wrath of God by experiencing the death we rightly deserve. His death propitiated (satisfied) that wrath, not because we are good or because we try hard, but because He loves us (I John 4:9, 10) and because His justice requires a payment for sin (Romans 3:25). For those who accept

Christ's payment for their sins, God's wrath is forever satisfied, and "God has poured out His love into our hearts" (Romans 5:5, NIV). Instead of living in fear and condemnation, we become His dearly beloved children in whom He delights!

Security factor #2: Justification

Justification refers to God's forgiving everything we've done wrong and declaring us as having done everything right. Most of us cannot believe God is able to view us as having done everything right until we are really convinced that He has forgiven everything we've done wrong.

Paul describes a graphic picture of God's forgiveness:

When you were dead in your sins and in the uncircumcision of your sinful nature, God made you alive with Christ. He forgave us all our sins, having canceled the written code, with its regulations, that was against us and that stood opposed to us; He took it away, nailing it to the cross (Colossians 2:13, 14, NIV).

The imagery in these verses is derived from the practice that controlled legal indebtedness. The certificate of debt is a document signed by the debtor acknowledging a legal IOU. Obviously, none of us can repay the debt that Jesus paid on our behalf. So this certificate of debt becomes something which is hostile to our interests and for which we need forgiveness!

Paul says that Jesus did two things to that document. It was: (1) taken away [by being blotted out], and (2) nailed to His cross. The words *took it away* portray force. The removal was not timidly done. The word *canceled* denotes a "blotting or rubbing out," the way that writing on official records was removed. God has wiped the slate clean—with vigor. "I [the Lord] am He who blots out your transgressions, for My own sake, and remembers your sins no more" (Isaiah 43:25, NIV).

Jesus also nailed the certificate of debt to the cross. Paul's words may refer to the custom of nailing the inscription of a guilty person's crime on his cross (Mark 15:26). God nailed the accusation against each of us to the cross of Jesus. When Jesus uttered, "It is finished," not only was His work done on earth, but our debt was ended as well.

Jesus forgave our debt *and* destroyed the paper upon which it was recorded. Our sins have been paid for. We are completely forgiven. And we have been granted the legal status of righteousness before God (II Corinthians 5:21). This liberating truth should free us from haunting guilt and compel us to live wholeheartedly for Him who sets us free.

Security factor #3: Reconciliation

The word *reconcile* means to make enemies into friends. We were enemies of God (Romans 5:10), separated from Him because of sin. But Christ's blood is the payment for the sin which caused our alienation. Now we can become reconciled to God and be totally accepted by Him! This truth of reconciliation is clearly seen in Colossians 1:19-22 (*NIV*):

God was pleased to have all His fullness dwell in Him [Jesus], and through Him to reconcile to Himself all things, whether things on earth or things in heaven, by making peace through His blood, shed on the cross. Once you were alienated from God and were enemies in your minds because of your evil behavior. But now He has reconciled you by Christ's physical body through death to present you holy in His sight, without blemish and free from accusation.

This passage describes those apart from Christ as alienated and hostile in mind, engaged in evil deeds. Such a description might summon up images of people such as Hitler, Stalin, the Ayatollah Khomeini, Idi Amin, and Mohamar Khadafy. It is easy to think of *them* as alienated, hostile, and evil. Yet the same description accurately describes us before we trusted Christ as Savior.

God's unconditional acceptance of us supersedes all other relationships. "If God is for us, who can be against us?" (Romans 8:31, NIV). Even if all others laugh at us, desert us, or ridicule us, we have a faithful friend. Jesus remains closer than a brother. He understands us completely and accepts us totally.

We live securely in the unconditional love, forgiveness, and acceptance of God because of Jesus' substitutionary death on our behalf. Our security is firmly founded; our purpose springs out of these truths. Since Christ has done so much for us, we want to honor Him. In fact, our passion and intensity for Christ are expressed in the clear purpose statement: "We have as our ambition . . . to be pleasing to Him" (II Corinthians 5:9).

I used to think ambition was always selfish. But when I read this passage one day, I realized that ambition is neutral. It becomes right or wrong depending on what a person is ambitious to obtain. Most people may have selfish ambitions, but it is possible to have an ambition that is pure and holy. Christ is the only One worthy of abject affection, hard work and day-dreams. It is right to be ambitious to honor Him.

[I highly recommend the book and workbook, *The Search for Significance,* by Robert McGee. The liberating truths of this chapter are explained in more detail in his book, and the workbook is a great help in applying them. For copies, write to *The Search for Significance,* 8876 Gulf Freeway, Suite 340, Houston, Texas 77017.]

The significance trapeze

God's unconditional love, forgiveness, and acceptance are attractive, yet some of us are hesitant to respond to them. Walter Trobisch explains that we are like a man holding on to a trapeze bar, swinging high in the circus tent. He knows he must let go of the bar he's holding to grab the other one. Grabbing the other bar is an act of the will, based on the knowledge that it will hold him up and take him to the other platform.

In the same way, some of us want to hold on to our performance and our abilities to please others even though they won't take us where we need to go. We need to be convinced that God's love, forgiveness, and acceptance are indeed real. Then we need to let go and, as an act of will, grab the new bar. We need to transfer our trust from ourselves to Jesus.

My job involves a lot of public speaking. I have vivid memories of my first attempts to communicate to large crowds (any group of more than two people). I prepared like crazy, attempting to cram everything I knew about the subject into a 35-minute slot. Feedback was something I both dreaded and longed for, depending on whether it was negative or positive.

On one occasion, my talk had gone just as I had hoped. A colleague was doing a critique of my efforts, and as she walked up, I was eager to hear her praise. Terry (who is usually so perceptive) proceeded to rip my talk to shreds in her own gentle way. When she was through, I wondered if I had done *anything* well. I was devastated! My self-worth, based solidly on my performance and others' opinions, was shot.

Through the years I have been learning to let go of the trapeze bar of performance and grab the bar of God's unconditional love and acceptance. This transfer occurs as I allow God's opinion of me to become more important than the opinions of others.

Such a transfer of trust has had an impact on my public speaking. My focus is slowly shifting, from myself and my ability to speak, to the people in the audience. I value people's appreciation, but I'm learning that my self-worth does not depend on their approval. I have a long way to go, but these changes are a mark of God's grace, and I am thankful.

Our culture has a high view of man and a low view of God. Man is perceived as central, with all other things existing for his pleasure. God (if He is acknowledged at all) is thought of as a somewhat senile but kindly grandfather who isn't in

control of Himself, let alone the universe. This exalted view of
man is commonly labeled *humanism*, and has its roots in the
Renaissance and Enlightenment periods.

Thomas Jefferson was one of the giants of the Enlightenment era. He was a genius in many areas, but not in theology.
He was a deist who believed that God created the world and
then bade it good-bye. God, he surmised, was no longer interested in the affairs of men, much less in control of them.

When Jefferson read the Bible, he found doctrines like
the deity of Christ that didn't correspond with his beliefs, but
this wasn't a problem for a man of his creativity. He simply cut
out the passages he didn't agree with. The Jefferson Bible has
been used by "enlightened" people since his day. It contains the
four Gospels, but deletes every reference to Christ's deity. Each
Gospel ends at the crucifixion. The reader is left with a Jesus
who was a very nice, but sadly misunderstood man who died at
the hands of His enemies and remained a corpse. There is no
forgiveness, no hope, and no living Savior. According to Jefferson, man doesn't need God. He can make it on his own.

Humanism today has the same impact. Its effect on theology, and specifically on the grace of God, is staggering. Most
humanists teach that man is basically good. If the existence of
Christ is recognized, it is as an example of what man is capable
of doing. But the idea that Jesus is the sovereign Lord is a
threat to the exalted view of man.

Often, the "gospel" is communicated in a way that states
in effect, "Man is basically good and Jesus helps us be a little
better." It is as if we are at a negative .01 on a continuum and
Jesus nudges us over the zero point to a plus .01.

But as we have seen, this is tantamount to heresy. Apart
from Christ, man is alienated, an enemy of God, a helpless and
hopeless sinner. His position is fixed infinitely on the negative
side of the spectrum. But through the grace of God, he need
not remain there. And God's grace doesn't take us only to plus

.01 on the spectrum. We have been made *children* of God, *coheirs* with Christ, indwelt by the very Spirit of God.

The following diagram illustrates the contrast between humanism's paltry view of grace with the true grace of God.

Errant View of Grace

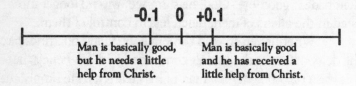

-0.1   0   +0.1

Man is basically good, but he needs a little help from Christ.

Man is basically good and he has received a little help from Christ.

Biblical View of Grace

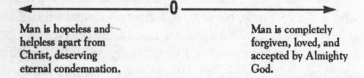

0

Man is hopeless and helpless apart from Christ, deserving eternal condemnation.

Man is completely forgiven, loved, and accepted by Almighty God.

Which of these diagrams is closer to your view of God's grace? Your answer will determine how much you value Christ's gracious payment for your sins and how much you still cling to your own abilities to perform and please others.

Making the Gospel trivial?

In his book, *People of the Lie*, Scott Peck says that because so many people in our culture (including Christians) believe in the inherent goodness of man, we have a weak view of sin and the wrath of God. We make the Gospel trivial, using it as little more than a self-help tool to make good people a little better. We desperately need a clear biblical view of the sin and evil which are devastating lives now and will have dire consequences for eternity.

An exalted view of man and corresponding low view of God also affects our perception of what we deserve. A combination of humanism and media influence makes it easy for us to believe that we have the right to success, comfort, and approval, so we pursue these things with a righteous intensity.

Whenever we accomplish goals, we expect to be rewarded. When we have been a good son or daughter, friend, spouse, or employee, we think we deserve to be treated well and appreciated. When we look nice, we anticipate compliments.

But the only thing we really deserve is hell! Because of our rebellion against God and our desires for independence and honor, we deserve His condemnation. It is only by God's free gift of grace that we have been rescued from such an awful fate.

We tend to compare our lives with the Hollywood image of beauty, money, comfort, respect, and excitement, which always leads to dissatisfaction. We need to compare our lives with what we actually deserve (hell) instead of what we think we deserve (Hollywood). Then we can find contentment and peace, and we will value the right things.

As I spoke on this topic at a conference, a statement came to mind that capsulizes this idea: "Anything that happens to us that is better than hell is by God's grace." Immediately after I spoke, it was time for lunch. Typical of conferences, the lunch menu consisted of mystery meat, concrete potato blobs, and marbles disguised as peas. "Well," somebody said, "it's better than hell!" That statement in that context gave us a fresh perspective. Instead of griping about the lunch, we became somewhat more satisfied.

The better-than-hell concept has encouraged me to be content many times when I have been tempted to complain. (However, we had to stop saying, "It's better than hell" around the children. We were afraid they would go to their preschool class, not be able to draw or play with blocks, and say, "Well, Mrs. Norris, I guess it's better than hell!")

The good life vs. abundant life

Why do we have this problem of believing we deserve comfort, success, and recognition? It is because we have confused the good life with the abundant life that Christ promised (John 10:10). The good life connotes pleasant circumstances: enough pleasure, enough money, and enough approval from others to make us free from want (though we seem to always want more). Is this the abundant life Jesus promised us?

In the Scriptures, "life" and "the abundant life" are characterized by three attributes: purpose, sacrifice, and contentment. These things are directly contradictory to what we call "the good life." As we have seen, most people's purposes are very self-centered, but in the abundant life, a person's purpose is to honor Christ no matter what the personal cost. Jesus said:

If anyone would come after Me, he must deny himself and take up his cross and follow Me. For whoever wants to save his life will lose it, but whoever loses his life for Me will find it (Matthew 16:24, 25, NIV).

Sacrifice is far from the minds of those seeking the good life. Such people may willingly endure *some* hardships, but it is usually for their own eventual gain, like a businessman who works hard so he can take a long vacation or get a promotion. That is hardly sacrifice! Jesus showed us what true sacrifice is:

This is how we know what love is: Jesus Christ laid down His life for us. And we ought to lay down our lives for our brothers. If anyone has material possessions and sees his brother in need but has no pity on him, how can the love of God be in him? Dear children, let us not love with words or tongue but with actions and in truth (I John 3:16-18, NIV).

True contentment is not having an abundance of money, possessions, and friends. Rather, genuine commitment comes from being satisfied with Christ and with what He provides to meet our needs—not all our wants.

Paul explained the basis of contentment to Timothy:
Godliness with contentment is great gain. For we
brought nothing into the world, and we can take
nothing out of it. But if we have food and clothing,
we will be content with that. People who want to get
rich fall into temptation and a trap and into many
foolish and harmful desires that plunge men into ruin
and destruction (I Timothy 6:6-9, *NIV*).

Class reunion

Every year at Christmas, Juliana had a party so that all of
us who graduated together could catch up on the events of the
previous year. The first year, a lot of people were in graduate
school, law school, or medical school. I was asked, "Didn't you
go on the staff of Campus Crusade for Christ?" I answered,
"Yes, I sure did," but somehow it didn't sound impressive.

By the fourth year, my classmates were advancing in
their chosen fields. A couple of them were in their residencies,
several had joined law practices, and one or two were getting
Ph.D.'s in biochemical engineering or other impressive-
sounding fields. "And what are you doing now, Pat?" someone
would ask. "Oh, I'm still with Campus Crusade for Christ," I'd
gather the courage to say boldly.

By the eighth year, my classmates were excelling. One
had received a fellowship at Duke Medical School, a couple of
lawyers had been made partners in their firms, and one was a
professor at a prestigious university. Several were talking about
their fine homes and extravagant vacations.

The inevitable question came: "Pat, are you still with
Campers Crusades or whatever it is?" I wanted to say smugly,
"No, I'm getting my third doctorate in astrobiological geo-
physics of Medieval literature." But I had to say, "It's called
Campus Crusade, and yes, I'm still with them."

I didn't feel very content with God's will for my life

when my friends seemed to have so much more prestige and prosperity. It was time for me to do more serious reflecting.

Purpose, sacrifice, and contentment are characteristics of the abundant life. Jesus promises us these things, but not everything on every television commercial. Abundant life is characterized more by obedience than by material blessings.

Security and significance become ours as we receive the unconditional love and acceptance of Christ. He rescues us from the slavery and condemnation we deserve and gives us what the world longs for but can't seem to find: love, forgiveness, and purpose.

Dr. John Hannah, a professor at Dallas Theological Seminary, says that the Christian life is "obedience out of gratitude." More of us need to make this our goal as we respond to what God has done for us.

QUESTIONS

1. *What are some reasons people give for holding onto success, happiness, and approval instead of receiving Christ's wonderful love, forgiveness, and acceptance?*

2. *What are some sources that communicate the message: "Man is basically good"?*

3. *How would your attitudes and actions be different if you were gripped with the fact that "anything that is better than hell is by God's grace"?*

4. *Have you confused "the good life" with "the abundant life"? If so, how?*

5. *Read Romans 5:6-11 and Colossians 1:19-22. How are people separated from Christ described in these passages? What has God done for us? How was it accomplished?*

Chapter 13
Choosing Generosity

I first met Kyle when he was a sophomore at the University of Missouri. He's warm, likable, and spunky—the sort of person who never met a stranger. We were in a Bible study group together, and I could tell by his enthusiasm about the Lord that there was a lot of potential in this young man. But too often "potential" proves to be an expendable commodity. Many enthusiastic young Christians go up like a rocket and come down like a rock. Would Kyle's zeal for God go down the tubes when he got out of college?

After graduation, Kyle went to work for a bank in a small farming community in northern Missouri. His infectious enthusiasm was coupled with good sense, and he got promoted rapidly. By the time he was twenty-seven years old, he had become the bank's president—a position that most of his peers would strive for all their lives.

Yet the bank did not consume all of Kyle's time. His family and his ministry were top priorities. He had married a girl named Donna and they were raising a family based on biblical principles. They were also active leaders in their church and other outreach programs. In fact, Kyle's ministry at a nearby prison resulted in scores of inmates accepting Christ, and the men and women Kyle and his wife discipled received genuine care and attention, not just a quick and superficial hour a week. It seemed to be an ideal life: a wonderful family, an effective ministry, and the prestige of being a young bank president.

Kyle was doing such a good job that the bank owner bought another one and asked Kyle to take it over and make it profitable. The bank had been mismanaged and had a number of bad loans that needed to be written off. But when Kyle finished an audit of the bank's outstanding loan portfolio, he found that the previous owners had miscalculated slightly.

Kyle stood before a bank board of inquiry in St. Louis (a young, baby-faced executive in front of a group of surly, cynical, veteran bank examiners) and told them that the $150,000 in bad loans reported by the previous owners was actually closer to $1,500,000! The board members were surprised, but as they examined the facts, they discovered Kyle was right.

Kyle had saved his boss more than a million dollars. He was a hero. He reveled in the power he was acquiring, and he became more and more interested in the source of this prestige and power: money.

A few months later, Kyle's boss made another offer. He would buy a series of banks every eighteen months or so for Kyle to make profitable. Kyle would receive 30% of the stock, 100% financed. The dividends would be used to pay off the note. That would give him about $500,000 for each bank, in addition to his salary. But there was one string attached. Until the notes were fully paid, Kyle would be locked in, required to jump anytime his boss said "jump." It was a fabulous offer for anyone who wanted to get rich quick. The power and the opportunities for wealth absorbed Kyle.

Every morning for years, he had meditated on Psalm 19:14: "Let the words of my mouth and the meditation of my heart be acceptable in Thy sight, O Lord, my rock and my Redeemer." But as making money increasingly occupied his time and attention, Kyle made a startling discovery. He wasn't thinking about the Lord anymore.

I happened to call Kyle during this period of his life to see how he and his wife were doing. He told me that the increasing time he was spending at the bank was seriously affecting his family life and his ministry. He told me, "I got sucked in and I didn't even know it. I began to work so long and so hard to make money that I don't even remember a significant period of growth in my children's lives. I wasn't there to notice. I was at the bank." His wife finally told him, "I would rather have you take a job with half the salary you make now than to continue this life-style!"

Kyle had some hard choices to make, and he courageously chose what very few people are willing to do. He resigned from the prestigious position as bank president and the promise of wealth. Instead, he took a lower position at less pay so he could devote more time to his family and ministry.

He didn't run out. He finished the job of restructuring the bank's loans before he left. But he would not allow a career to interfere with what was important to him. Kyle's biblical priorities were not just theoretical. They were real.

A different agenda

Many of us say we follow Christ. But when the choice must be made between advancing our careers or advancing our families and ministries, we opt for the career with only a brief twinge of guilt. Yet God's grace is a powerful motivation. When we begin to grasp the significance of His unconditional love and acceptance, one of the areas that begins to change is stewardship—how we spend our money and our time.

The principle of stewardship helps us put shoe leather to our values. If Christ is Lord, then everything we have belongs to Him. We are stewards, not owners, of our things. The realization that we will someday stand before Christ and give a full accounting for all He entrusts to us should make a tremendous difference in how we use our money and possessions.

It is one thing to espouse biblical values. It is quite another to have the guts to make the right choices. Jesus said, "Why do you call Me, 'Lord, Lord,' and do not do what I say?" (Luke 6:46). His clear implication is that we should either do what He says or stop calling Him "Lord." It is nonsense to call Him "Lord" while pursuing our own agendas of comfort, affluence, and prestige.

But how can we know if we are pursuing our own agenda or Christ's? You'll see what you really value by examining how you spend your money and your time. In this chapter and the next one, we will examine these two windows on our value systems.

In the week before His crucifixion, Jesus spent a lot of time with His disciples in the temple. One day they sat and watched those who were putting contributions into the temple treasury. Jesus used this instance to teach a profound lesson about giving:

> Jesus sat down opposite the place where the offerings were put and watched the crowd putting their money into the temple treasury. Many rich people threw in large amounts. But a poor widow came and put in two very small copper coins, worth only a fraction of a penny. Calling His disciples to Him, Jesus said, "I tell you the truth, this poor widow has put more into the treasury than all the others. They all gave out of their wealth; but she, out of her poverty, put in everything—all she had to live on" (Mark 12:41-44, NIV).

While the disciples watched the woman putting her coins in the treasury and heard Jesus' words, two questions may have come to mind: "How much should I give?" and "Why should I give?"

How much a person was to give was not in question in Jesus' day. The tithe, usually considered today to be one-tenth of a person's income, was actually two separate gifts of one-tenth plus various other contributions (for a combined total of about 22% of the person's income—see Leviticus 27:30; Deuteronomy 14:22; and Psalm 50:14).

In the New Testament, the tithe is found only in references of Old Testament illustrations, not in direct instructions to believers. In the covenant of grace, there is the perspective that everything we have is the Lord's, and we should use it all to honor Him and help others. (Honoring Him obviously involves providing for the basic needs of ourselves and our families as well as contributing to meet the needs of others.)

There is no dichotomy between what is God's and what is mine. As we understand more and more of God's unconditional love and power, giving becomes a joy instead of a resented obligation.

All you can spare

C. S. Lewis was a brilliant author who made enough money from the sale of his books to live well. However, he lived modestly in an old home with creaking floors. He was generous with his money, contributing about two-thirds of it to help meet various needs. When someone asked him how much a person should give away, Lewis replied succinctly yet profoundly, "All you can spare."

Lewis's life-style was characterized by generosity. Too often, our life-styles are characterized by acquisitions. We spend exorbitant amounts of time, effort, and money to accumulate more (while our closets and garages already bulge). Instead of *acquiring* all we possibly can, our attitude should be to *give* all we possibly can. How much should we give? All we can spare.

The next logical question is: *Why* should a person give? There are many good reasons: appreciation, compassion, and stewardship to list a few. But perhaps most important is the sheer joy of giving.

Before last Christmas, Catherine, my 5-year-old daughter, asked me, "Daddy, what am I going to get for Christmas?"

I explained to her, "Christmas is about giving. God gave us His Son, and the wise men gave Him gifts. Let's think of what you can give instead of what you will get."

Catherine quickly responded and got excited about what she could get for her friend, Meredith. On Christmas morning, we all went into the living room and opened presents around the tree. Catherine enjoyed all the presents she received, but she was more excited about the presents she had bought or made for other people.

Seeing the needs of other people often compels us to give. When I traveled to India and Thailand last spring, I saw many of the effects of the ministry of Campus Crusade for Christ. In a village near Bangalore, India, we saw many people accept Christ after watching the film *Jesus* in their native language. We met a young man whose life had been threatened by Sikhs in the Punjab a few months before; he was returning there to be light and salt in that violent part of the world. We visited a leper colony where we sang a few songs at a church begun by Campus Crusade's ministry. We toured a stinking slum and heard stories of hundreds who had come to Christ there. We saw a dead Moslem man being washed on the side of the street. The needs we saw were enormous.

Thomas Abraham, Campus Crusade's director for Central Asia and the Pacific, told me there are 303 staff positions in India. The good news was that last year, 287 fully qualified Indians applied for those positions. But the bad news was that only eight of them could be accepted because no more funds were available. The salary for a missionary family in India with Campus Crusade is only $50 to $60 a month, but it is exceptionally difficult to raise financial support in a country where only the lowest caste, the untouchables, ask for money.

Here was an opportunity to almost double CCC's missionary staff in India, but only eight people could be added. And the need is so small for each person! One young man I met, Eepan, needed only $55 a month for his support. Because of the things we had seen, Joyce and I determined to be a part of the solution.

When I returned from the trip, I needed a pair of tennis shoes, so I went to a discount sporting goods store and bought a nice leather pair on sale for $27. After I paid for them it struck me that the price of these shoes represented half of Eepan's monthly support! Half! The reality of opulence in America (and in my life) became more apparent than ever before.

Since then, I have often compared the price of my purchases to Eepan's need. Fifty dollars for a week's groceries would pay for almost all of Eepan's housing, food, clothes, transportation, and ministry needs for a month. Eepan has made me more aware of where my money goes—and where it *could* go.

This comparison may seem extreme to some people. It may even seem legalistic. But it is only legalistic if we give out of guilt and obligation. It is reasonable to reflect on all that God has done for us. Then, out of appreciation, we can consider how to give more to help people in other parts of the world. We can give compassionately and cheerfully, not grudgingly.

We become compelled to give as we realize that if we don't help, others won't be able to do what God has called them to do. In God's plan, our abundance is meant to supply others in need. As the Scriptures say, "He who gathered much did not have too much, and he who gathered little had no lack" (II Corinthians 8:15).

Not all giving is based on pure motives. Some Christian leaders promote giving in order to get more, citing various promises in the Scriptures. But the Bible provides no timetable or method by which God will bless us for our giving. In this self-seeking, prosperous age, it is wiser to focus on developing other characteristics of giving: cheerfulness (II Corinthians 9:7), generosity (Romans 12:8, *NIV*), secrecy (Matthew 6:1-4), and expecting nothing in return (Luke 6:35).

Acts of righteousness

In his book, *Idols for Destruction*, Herbert Schlossberg states that most people give out of the self-centered desire for power and control over the one who receives their help. The craving to be respected and appreciated is also selfish, and therefore, an impure reason for giving.

Jack is a friend of mine who received a sizable inheritance a few years ago. For a while he had a dream of giving away $100 million in his lifetime. He would lie awake at night thinking of causes he could champion and needs he could meet, and he believed God would bless him for his generosity.

Then the Lord began to show Jack his true motive. Driving alone on an interstate highway one day, he realized he was motivated by the desire to be powerful and admired by others. Giving large sums of money was a means to that end.

His dreams of self-glory and of receiving praise from people began to fade. Now a simple and pure devotion to Christ is evident in Jack's giving. In the joy of giving, Jack has discovered true generosity.

Jack learned that God doesn't value the magnitude of the gift. The amount is important only in relation to a person's net worth. For instance, the widow in the temple gave only a few cents, but it was of great worth because it was all she had.

I learned a lesson about comparable worth when my great aunt died and left part of her estate to my mother. Aunt

Addie Sue had lived in a large, beautiful home on a mountain overlooking the picturesque little city of Rome, Georgia. Uncle Will had designed the house himself. It had a Jeffersonian flair: hidden closets, a multiple-use deck, high ceilings, and beautiful views. Addie Sue had furnished it with some of the finest antiques I have ever seen. We drove to Rome from my parents' home in Gainesville, Georgia, and loaded a U-Haul truck with beautiful furniture: a 12′ x 18′ antique Oriental rug, a pier mirror and table, a four-poster bed made in the 1770's, lamps, chairs, silver, paintings, and all kinds of other furnishings.

As I drove the truck back to Gainesville, I decided to stop at the old family farmhouse. The run-down dogtrot house had become something of a one-family geriatric commune. Mr. Evans was renting the place, living there with two sisters and a retarded cousin. The youngest of the bunch was about seventy, and all four of them lived on Mr. Evans's retirement pension. They were poor, but they loved the Lord, and the sisters had planted so many flowers that the place looked like a postcard.

As I pulled in the driveway off the dirt road, I could see all four of them sitting on the porch. When they recognized me, Lizzy quickly ran inside to put her teeth in. (She would be very embarrassed for me to see her without them.) We sat on the porch and talked for a while. Ruby excitedly showed me the big white family Bible her sister had given her last Christmas. Mr. Evans told me about the neighbor's cattle, and Roy showed me the wood he had chopped. It was a thoroughly delightful time with these kind and simple people.

As I got up to leave, Lizzy and Ruby went in the house for a few seconds. When they returned, Mr. Evans said slowly, "Pat, the girls and Roy and me want to help you with your missionary work with Campus Crusade." Then he handed me a folded $10 bill. Lizzy and Ruby each grinned and gave me $5 bills that had been neatly folded four times, and then Roy gave me two crumpled dollar bills out of his pocket.

I stood motionless and mute for a few seconds trying to figure out how to give back these dear poor people their much needed money, but I realized that would insult them. I said only, "Thank you all very much. I really appreciate it." But my words were inadequate.

As soon as I got in the truck, the thought hit me: "This $22 is worth far more than all the thousands and thousands of dollars worth of antiques in the back!" These poor people had gladly given all they could possibly spare to help me. The significance of the widow's coins took on new and poignant meaning for me that day.

Why should we give? We should give out of appreciation for God's grace, because we want to help meet the needs of others, and because we will give an account to Christ for how we have used the resources He has entrusted to us.

How should we give? Cheerfully—not out of guilt or obligation. How much should we give? All we can spare.

QUESTIONS

1. *Do you think Kyle did the right thing when he took a cut in pay and a lower position so he could spend more time with his family and ministry? Why or why not?*

2. *How would your use of money be affected if you were convinced that all of it should be used to honor the Lord? Be specific.*

3. *Read Luke 19:12-27. How did the nobleman respond to each slave's stewardship? Which slave characterizes your life (your schedule, your budget, etc.)?*

Chapter 14
Choosing to Use Time Wisely

Betty Harragan, author of the career guide, *Games Mother Never Taught You*, has observed:

> Only three or four years ago, at many companies if you worked late it looked like you were incompetent, and just couldn't get your work done. Now, sixty hours is a normal workweek for many professionals.

Harragan cites the reason for the increased work load as an increasing number of baby boomers competing for fewer white-collar positions. But when you get right down to it, *our use of time reveals our true priorities*.

If we value success, comfort, and approval above all else, two problems result: we spend too much time and attention on some things and too little on others. We are stewards of the time God gives us, and we should use it to accomplish things of eternal value. Material possessions, titles, and prestige will perish, but three things are eternal: God, God's Word, and people. Our use of time should reflect those ongoing priorities.

Time for work

The relentless pursuit of career advancement is not only the accepted norm in our society, indeed it is considered a virtue. The pressure to move up the ladder is the driving force and top priority of many executives.

Hard work is not the villain here. The prestige of success is the real culprit. The purpose of our activities determines their worth. Hard work is honoring to the Lord—if it is done expressly for His honor.

Paul's challenge to the Colossian believers applies to us as well:

Whatever you do, work at it with all your heart, as working for the Lord, not for men (Colossians 3:23, NIV).

This instruction was addressed to slaves! If they were expected to remain focused on God rather than their masters, surely we can place more emphasis on pleasing God rather than our bosses.

Time for play

Leisure also competes for the precious time God has given us. There is nothing wrong with leisure, per se, but we need to control it. Watching hour after hour of television or spending an exorbitant amount of time on a hobby or sports needs to be evaluated.

Exercise and relaxation are gifts from the Lord to replenish our physical and emotional resources. Properly used, they are vital ingredients in our life-style of honoring Christ and building quality relationships with our families and others.

One age-old method of relaxation needs to be revived in our day—reading. It is not only relaxing; it stimulates as well. But books are too often laid aside in favor of the visually stimulating media today. Many television programs, videos, and movies do not require thought. And while "vegging out" may be convenient and effortless, it does little to stimulate a person intellectually.

Reading, on the other hand, can put you in touch with the great minds of today or any age in history. Through books you can deepen your reservoir of knowledge and develop appreciation of the incredible intricacies of life. For Christians, the principle of stewardship applies to all that God has entrusted to us, including our minds. As we develop intellectually, we will appreciate God and His creation more. We will also understand other people better and interact with them more intelligently.

Oswald Sanders emphasized the need to be well-read in his classic book, *Spiritual Leadership* (Moody Press). He wrote:

> The man who desires to grow spiritually and
> intellectually will be constantly at his books . . . .
> Today, the practice of reading solid and rewarding
> spiritual and classical literature is seriously on the
> wane. In an age in which people have more leisure
> than ever before in the history of the world, many
> claim that they have no time to read. This excuse is
> never valid with a spiritual leader.

Joyce and I understand the temptation to become "couch potatoes" only too well. After a long day of tending to children, cleaning, washing, attending various meetings, cooking, and getting the children ready for bed, Joyce is ready for some leisure. And after a long day of meetings, planning, endless phone calls about everything in the world, and helping with the children after I get home, a little vegging seems like a just reward for me.

The choices Joyce and I make during such times are very important (though they are often hard to make). We may choose to talk, play a game, or read. Occasionally we find a good movie or sports event on television, but we have made a pact not to watch mindless shows. We try not to be legalistic, but there just isn't much worth watching anymore.

Jesus has promised us rest, but His offer is much more profound than mere physical rest. He makes available the kind of rest that restores every aspect of our lives. True rest is not found in escape, but in the love and strength of Christ. Look closely at His invitation:

Come to Me, all you who are weary and burdened, and I will give you rest. Take My yoke upon you and learn from Me, for I am gentle and humble in heart, and you will find rest for your souls. For My yoke is easy and My burden is light (Matthew 11:28-30, NIV).

And just as we have a misperception of rest, we also have a similar problem with defining exercise. Yes, exercise has value since we are stewards of our health. But today's preoccupation with muscular bodies, perfect figures, and flawless complexions is far off the mark of biblical priorities.

Physical fitness is important, but not nearly as important as a strong spiritual life. Paul instructed Timothy regarding the balance of physical fitness and spiritual fitness:

Discipline yourself for the purpose of godliness; for bodily discipline is only of little profit, but godliness is profitable for all things, since it holds promise for the present life and also for the life to come (I Timothy 4:7, 8).

When activities such as work and leisure are overemphasized, other important aspects of our lives are neglected—and sometimes totally overlooked. As important as these things are, we must be careful not to eliminate another essential element of life—spiritual discipline.

Time for God

Most of us are long on good intentions but woefully short on discipline when it comes to reading the Scriptures and praying. We depend on church services or group Bible studies to provide spiritual nourishment. These are significant activities, of course, but there is no substitute for consistent personal times involved in learning from God's Word and meaningful prayer.

Some of us go through the motions of daily devotions, but it is rote activity. We don't experience the delight (and conviction) of discovering truth in the Scriptures, and we lack intimacy with the Lord as we pray. The issue is not *when* you have your time with the Lord, or *where*, or *how long* that time should be. The form is not important. The issue is intimacy with God and dependence on Him.

We may have a wide range of motivations in all of our "spiritual" activities (going to church, giving, prayer, evangelism, discipling, personal devotions, teaching, and so forth). We can participate out of guilt, obligation, or the desire to impress others. On the other hand, we can be involved because we want to know God better and serve Him more effectively.

Occasionally we will experience times when we need to obey God even when we don't feel like it. But there is no room for blindly following a religious form to earn the acceptance of God or of other people. Christianity should be based on a relationship, not a ritual.

A few years ago I was experiencing a period of spiritual dryness—yet another in an all-too-frequent series of them. I analyzed my life to the nth degree to discover what was wrong. I was diligent to read the Bible and pray, wasn't I? I was doing my best, wasn't I? Introspection yielded more discouragement.

Then the Lord put His finger on the problem—one I have already mentioned. My purpose in life, to be like Christ, focused attention on myself instead of Jesus. My questions were totally self-centered: "Have I changed since last month?" "How can I grow faster?" "Am I getting better than so-and-so?"

My goal was self-improvement, my standard was God Almighty, and my only resource was myself! No wonder my devotional life (as well as the rest of my life) was dry! Blech!

As my purpose shifted from myself to God, my devotional life improved. The issues of where, when, how, and how often became less important. My motivations of obligation and dread began to turn into desire to know God better. The Scriptures came alive for me—no longer a self-improvement manual, but a personal love letter to me from the compassionate God of the universe.

The redefinition of my purpose was a pivotal point. Since then, my times with the Lord have been far less dry and introspective, and much more full of thanksgiving and praise.

Time for family

Deceptive goals of success and comfort also put pressures on marriages, frequently with devastating effects. One out of two marriages ends in divorce, but that statistic cannot express the bitterness and pain experienced by children, spouses, relatives, and friends who share the hurt. And many marriages that stay intact are based on little more than a truce between combatants.

Parents who work extra hours to pay for the trappings of success also tend to neglect children. In such a home environment, the children also become absorbed with the demand for more and better things. And when the desire for more is greater than the ability to pay for it, debt adds to the emotional stress of the family.

Any marriage relationship is under tremendous pressure and must be protected and strengthened. Deep love and genuine understanding provide a strong base of security, but these do not develop by osmosis. Concerted effort and quality time is necessary before the marriage relationship can reflect the true beauty of our relationship with Christ (Ephesians 5:22-33).

Some mothers *must* work to support their families, but increasing numbers of moms work for the sole reason of providing extra income to support a better life-style. Dr. Burton

White, considered by many to be the world's foremost authority on early childhood development, has said that a child's self-esteem and stability is almost completely established by the time he or she is three years old. Dr. White states that a child must receive "irrational love" to develop a healthy self-esteem.

One has to ask: How many day-care workers, many of whom are overworked, give "irrational love" to the children they care for? Though their intentions may be pure, they simply cannot take the place of a loving parent. The price of our children's emotional instability is a staggering one compared to the extra dollars and pleasures earned when both parents work.

Some years ago a study indicated that the average American father spends *seventeen seconds* per day giving focused attention to each of his children. I thought that was an utterly reprehensible statistic—that is, until I became a father. Only then did realized how hard it is to do all a normal person has to do each day and still have the time and emotional energy to give focused attention to my children.

But who said we are supposed to be *normal?* We are to model behavior above the norm and do what God has instructed, not what our self-centered culture indicates is normal. We are to cherish and instruct our children (Deuteronomy 6). As gifts from the Lord, children should be a high priority rather than a hindrance to our personal goals.

Our values determine the way we spend our time, and the way we spend our time has a dramatic effect on family relationships.

Time for personal ministry

But when values are misplaced and time is spent in pursuit of the wrong things, family members aren't the only people who are cheated. After speaking at a conference on the topic of making the most of the time we have, a pastor told me about a board meeting at his church. As some of the board members arrived a little early, they began telling stories of their recent trout fishing trip to Colorado. They had planned for weeks, scouring maps to find the best trails to the best parts of the best streams. They had researched what kind of streamers and dry flies to use. They had bought food, oiled their boots, and borrowed a tent. In short, they had made sure that this fishing trip would be terrific, and it was!

They rode in Jeeps for several hours, hiked seven miles, and set up camp in one of those pristine mountain scenes usually reserved for postcards and beer commercials. Some of the men hadn't even unshouldered their packs when Jim's first cast hit the water. But they got those packs off in a hurry when they saw a fifteen-inch cutthroat jump to try to throw Jim's fly.

The men told story after story about their four-day trip, but then it was time for the meeting to start. The pastor spoke of problems the church was having in raising enough money for an addition to the Sunday school building. But when the chairman asked for volunteers to study the problem, there was silence. Since no one seemed to have the time or the energy, the job was left to the assistant pastor.

Later the topic moved to evangelism. Everyone was aware of the need to visit new people who attended church services and to train church members to share their faith. But again, when the pastor asked for someone to oversee this essential ministry, there was no response. Several men were specifically asked, including most of the ones who had been on the fishing trip. They all said they were sorry, but they just couldn't. The assistant pastor said he would do what he could.

It is a curious phenomenon when a Christian can be so excited, creative, and active about fishing, yet so numb and passive about reaching people for Christ. There is absolutely nothing wrong with a fishing trip. (I have some great fish stories of my own.) But we reveal a gross lack of understanding about eternal issues when we get so enthusiastic about a short-lived event while remaining so subdued about the prospect of men and women escaping eternal condemnation. People are worthy of far more planning, preparation, and energy than fish.

Participation in ministry takes time. A virile personal ministry almost inevitably involves commitment and personal sacrifice in terms of career advancement and the approval of others. We need to ask ourselves: Is it worth it?

And before you answer this question, remember that any sacrifice we make will be short-term. In light of eternity, any sacrifice for the glory of God will result in eternal rewards (which isn't a bad deal at all). Jesus promised:

Whoever wants to save his life will lose it, but whoever loses his life for Me will find it (Matthew 16:25, *NIV*).

Jim Elliot, a missionary to Ecuador, paraphrased Jesus' statement in his own words. His version was: "He is no fool who gives what he cannot keep to gain what he cannot lose." Elliot had a clear grasp of the wisdom of sacrifice. To him, sacrifice was the only reasonable option for the Christian. His firm belief was validated with his death—at the hands of the Auca Indians.

For each of us, a genuine commitment to Christ involves a life of sacrifice. Rick Amos, an engineer by vocation, also leads a campus ministry at the University of North Carolina at Wilmington. He stated perceptively,

There's a myth about full-time versus part-time ministry . . . that if you don't go full-time then you don't have to sacrifice as much. That's wrong! If you read what the Bible has to say, we need to have that same sacrificial mentality about everything as a full-time Christian worker.

I work forty to fifty hours a week, then I go to campus. Maybe my output isn't as great, but my attitude must be the same: that everything I have is the

Lord's. We must be completely available to God, and
we must be accountable to someone else so we will be
encouraged to keep going.

The grace of God and the Spirit of God produce changes
in our lives. Priorities are changed; affections are altered. We
become willing, then, to do what pleases Christ even if it is
inconvenient . . . even if others think we are foolish . . . even if
"everybody's doing it" all around us. We become willing to give
up some of our time to talk to someone else about Christ.

If these changes haven't taken place, then we probably
haven't grasped the liberating and compelling nature of God's
unconditional love and power. We need a better understanding
and a fresh experience of the love and forgiveness of God.
Then we become motivated to make these hard choices.

Rick is a friend of mine who graduated from Georgia
Tech at the top of his class in civil engineering. He was offered
an excellent job in his field, but he chose to join the staff of
Campus Crusade for Christ. A few months ago I visited him at
his home in Houston.

As I looked around, I noticed his diploma. The small
letters read "Summa Cum Laude." I told him, "Rick, I didn't
know you graduated with highest honors from Tech! If this
diploma were mine, I'd have lights flashing on it with a magni-
fying glass on the Summa Cum Laude and a Latin dictionary
nearby in case anybody needed it!"

Rick could be making six times his salary. He could easily
be haughty about his academic accomplishments and engineering superiority. He sacrificed the prestige, wealth, and comfort
that he could have had as an engineer. Yet to him it was no real
sacrifice. He is more concerned about Christ's honor than his
own. He is more concerned with the needs of others than his
own comfort and prosperity.

Has Rick made sacrifices for God? It depends on whom
you ask. Rick probably hasn't thought about it lately.

Does God want us to be successful, comfortable, and appreciated? The question is irrelevant. God *does* want us to respond to His grace, love Him with all our hearts, and live wholeheartedly for Him because He is worthy. If He gives us success, comfort, and recognition, fine. If not, that's fine, too.

Dr. Howard Hendricks, a professor at Dallas Theological Seminary, was talking to a wealthy businessman who confided, "All my life I've climbed the ladder of success, but when I got to the top, I found it was leaning against the wrong wall." What a sad commentary on the values of our culture!

What wall is your ladder leaning against? Where is your use of time and money leading you?

QUESTIONS

1. *List the TV programs you regularly watch. What is the message of each one?*

2. *What might be a better use of time than watching TV?*

3. *Make a list of books you would like to read.*

4. *What is your career goal? What are the probable consequences for your schedule, priorities, family, relationship with Christ, and personal ministry?*

5. *What is the goal of your devotional life? How would your relationship with God be affected if your goal was knowing and loving Christ?*

6. *How can you spend more quality time with your family? With your ministry?*

7. *What activities do you spend too much time on? What important activities do you tend to overlook? Write down specific steps for change.*

Chapter 15
Decisions that Change Lives

We can serve Christ in many ways. The body of Christ is designed to allow each person to function with his unique gifts and abilities, focused on the Lord and on relationships of grace and truth. But recently there has been an alarming trend toward focusing on programs instead of people. Administrative support roles are proliferating, taking precedence over the cutting-edge ministries of evangelism, discipleship, and prayer. That cutting edge needs to be sharpened and guarded.

At the University of Georgia, I played tennis almost every day. When I went to my first Campus Crusade for Christ meeting during my senior year, I saw someone I had seen on the courts a few days before. I was impressed with his game, so I introduced myself. His name was Tom. We talked about the game for a while, and he asked if I'd like to play sometime. "Sure," I replied immediately, "how about tomorrow?"

The next afternoon we met at the courts. We were evenly matched. As the games went by and the tension mounted, I began to get frustrated at every little mistake. I missed a drop shot and uttered a short expletive. Later I missed an overhead on a crucial point, after which an expletive was accompanied by a hurled projectile. (I cussed and threw my racket.) A few more similar incidents took place before the match ended. It had been close, and I can't even remember who won, but I remember that I was embarrassed. We had both been very competitive. Tom had kept his cool. I had lost all self-control.

I suspected that Tom would attempt a hasty exit. But to my surprise he came over, shook my hand, and said, "Let's go get a Coke." Instead of being offended by my temper, Tom was compassionate. The conversation we had after that tennis game started a long and deep friendship. He talked to me about the Lord, and asked if I wanted to play tennis again. I was startled, and I wasn't too sure if I wanted to, but I said yes.

Over the next several months, Tom and I spent many hours together. We visited each other, talked about everything imaginable, prayed together, studied the Bible together, and went to meetings together, but what I remember most are the times when Tom shared the Gospel with others as I tagged along. Sometimes we sat around tables in the Bulldog Room with five or six people. Tom answered question after question, and patiently explained the meaning of the cross of Christ. Sometimes we would be talking to someone in a class, and Tom would sensitively begin talking to him about Jesus.

He was a young man with guts. Once he attended a Gay Association meeting and waited until they asked if anybody had anything else to say. Tom got up, walked up to the front, and told the group of God's forgiveness and His power to change people. Some were outraged; some grumbled. But a few people asked to meet with Tom later. I had never met anyone else with the boldness and sensitivity to do things like that.

Prayer was not an isolated event in Tom's life. I remember praying together when several times I thought we were through, but Tom would continue praying for someone or some event. One autumn night, several people met outside to pray with Tom for an extended period. When they were through, everyone was chilled. Everybody, that is, but Tom. He was so intense about the needs of others and so intent on Christ, he hadn't even noticed how cold it was.

Tom was highly respected by other Christians on campus, but not because he held a title. Because of his zeal and effectiveness for Christ, he was often asked to take a leadership role in the organization. But he always said no. He didn't want to be encumbered by administrative responsibilities that would take time and attention away from his grass-roots, cutting-edge ministry of evangelism, discipleship, and prayer.

Tom and I did so many things together that we developed a very special friendship. I didn't realize until years later that he had discipled me. First and foremost, we were friends.

Choosing people over programs

I learned from Tom the importance of focusing on people instead of programs. We must never neglect the need for evangelism, discipleship, and prayer. Tom's action is a lasting example of the rewards of staying on the cutting edge.

Dale and Debbie are a couple who also protect their cutting-edge ministry. Dale is a computer scientist. Debbie is an artist who teaches oil painting. Both marshal their resources to honor Christ in every situation and every relationship. Both of them share the Gospel with their neighbors in Salt Lake City. Dale also talks to people in his office about Christ and leads a group of executives during lunch-hour Bible study through the Book of Romans.

Debbie's goal is to communicate the love and forgiveness of Christ to each person in every class she teaches. In an area where Christianity is not so prevalent, she has led a number of people to Christ and is discipling several of them.

Dale and Debbie could perform many administrative functions, but they believe God wants them in a cutting-edge ministry.

What is the biblical model for Christian service? Is it the administration of programs, or is it grass-roots evangelism, discipleship, and prayer? Think of a large farm in California, Texas, or Florida where fruits or vegetables are grown. When it is time to pick the crop, buses bring hundreds of laborers to do the picking. A few overseers are on hand to make sure the workers know where to pick. And in an office, somewhere, someone has made arrangements to hire the laborers and sell the crop. This farm is a model of Christians serving the Lord in the world. Jesus said, "The harvest is plentiful, but the workers are few. Therefore beseech the Lord of the harvest to send out workers into His harvest" (Matthew 9:37, 38). It is laborers we are lacking, who are so desperately needed.

But a more accurate picture of the church today would show a crop ready for harvest, with only a few overworked laborers doing the picking. There would be lots of committees analyzing how crops should be picked, how to select laborers, and what to do with the crop after it is picked. There would be an overseer (or two) for every laborer. Next to the last furrow would be grandstands where thousands of onlookers could watch the few sweating laborers. At lunch the gallery would descend like vultures on a few rows of picnic tables filled with ham and potato salad. They would enjoy eating and chatting with the overseers.

The church certainly needs gifted administrators and overseers for the ministry, but we are developing a host of man-agers instead of shepherds and evangelists. The proliferation of administrative roles takes people away from the much needed grass-roots ministry and involves them in programs (Sunday school, committees, banquets, fellowships, etc.). These pro-grams can be excellent vehicles for a grass-roots ministry, but often they are set up in a way that hinders that kind of ministry. Let's examine some biblical models for evangelism, discipleship, and prayer.

Choosing to evangelize

Everywhere Paul went, he told people about Jesus. He spoke to individuals, and he spoke to whole cities. He spoke to receptive people, and he spoke to those who despised him and tried to kill him. But whatever the response, he kept telling people about Christ. Paul's commitment to evangelism was intense:

> We proclaim Him, admonishing and teaching
> everyone with all wisdom, so that we may present
> everyone perfect in Christ. To this end I labor,
> struggling with all His energy, which so powerfully
> works in me (Colossians 1:28, 29, _NIV_).

Paul was gripped with the message that only Christ can forgive and make new. And he was gripped with the desperate needs of people. He understood that there is a supernatural, cosmic battle for the souls of men and women, and that Satan "has blinded the minds of the unbelieving, that they might not see the light of the gospel of the glory of Christ" (II Corinthians 4:4). He was so convinced of the power of Jesus and the needs of people that he would even give up his salvation if that were possible (Romans 9:1-3) to tell them about the Savior. His goal was to tell every person the Good News and then to help those who respond grow to maturity in Christ.

A couple of years ago I did some painful reflection on why I wasn't sharing my faith more. For many people, the fear of rejection is the chief factor that hinders them. But I came to the horrible conclusion that the reason I wasn't talking to more people about Christ was that evangelism was inconvenient. I was too busy with my own goals and schedules. Inconvenient?! How selfish! But the more I focus on the unconditional forgiveness of Christ and the fact that I really deserve hell, the more I find myself talking to more and more people about Him.

The question for me is not *if* I should share my faith, or *how* I can do it so I will feel comfortable. The question is, "How can I tell the most people so they will understand and repent?"

Recently, the Billy Graham organization held a conference in Amsterdam for evangelists from all over the world. A friend of mine who attended said his heart was stirred by the radical, selfless commitment of barefoot evangelists from Third World countries. Some had never owned a pair of shoes and were thrilled to have a pair—even if the shoes were of different sizes. Others were given ten pieces of clothes, and they put on all ten at the same time, wearing the bulky conglomeration for the entire conference. These men and women were giving up everything for the Gospel. In the face of such zeal, we must ask ourselves: "How much has success, pleasure, and approval deadened our willingness to live wholeheartedly for Christ?"

Those barefoot evangelists are living testimony of Paul's admonishment to Timothy:

Endure hardship with us like a good soldier of
Christ Jesus. No one serving as a soldier gets involved
in civilian affairs—he wants to please his command-
ing officer (II Timothy 2:3, 4, *NIV*).

The biblical model of evangelism is to sensitively and graciously tell everyone who will listen about Christ. Many activities may honor God, but fruitful evangelism makes the angels sing for joy!

For most of us, evangelism is a very frightening and threatening thing to consider. We are afraid of saying something stupid or of being rejected. It takes up our precious time and causes us some inconvenience. Evangelism *is* a struggle—the enemy certainly doesn't want us to do it. But it's not all that hard to at least get into a conversation with someone and tell them how you became a believer. That's a good start!

Choosing to disciple others

In our instant success culture, discipleship is sometimes reduced to handing someone a set of books and workbooks. While these materials can be helpful, they don't constitute effective discipleship. Biblical discipleship takes time, and it takes genuine love—the kind that Tom demonstrated to me.

Jesus spent a large quantity of time with His disciples: night and day for three years. And the quality of that time surely boggled the minds of the disciples. They saw Him teach, raise the dead, argue with hostile religious leaders, and demonstrate the deep truths of God.

The apostle Paul illustrated discipleship with a powerful and endearing metaphor of a mother with her child:

As apostles of Christ we could have been a burden
to you, but we were gentle among you, like a mother
caring for her little children. We loved you so much
that we were delighted to share with you not only the
gospel of God but our lives as well, because you had
become so dear to us. Surely you remember, brothers,
our toil and hardship; we worked night and day in
order not to be a burden to anyone while we preached
the gospel of God to you (I Thessalonians 2:6-9, _NIV_).

The meaning of this passage took on far greater depth as I watched Joyce nurse our children when they were babies. She lovingly met their needs, feeding them often while she sang or talked softly to them. Her tenderness and delight in them was evident. That picture of discipleship is a far cry from the "go through this booklet" mentality.

Steve and Sandi lived across the street from us a few years ago. One year, Steve invited each of the students he discipled to live in their home for a week, where they saw the household in all its glory: messy diapers, dirty dishes, understanding, and compassion. After a busy day when the children were asleep, the talks with Steve and Sandi were deeper and more intimate than some of these students had ever had before. The time spent with the students proved to be so influential that Steve and Sandi decided to invite people to visit on a regular basis. It's inconvenient at times, of course, but the benefits in the lives of the young students far outweigh the inconveniences.

Biblical discipleship involves the transfer of values and life-styles to another person in an environment of strong love and acceptance. It takes time, willingness, and security to be vulnerable about the realities of life—both the struggles and the victories. May more of us make such an effort!

Choosing to pray

Prayer is an expression of dependence on God. It is not practiced for very long by self-sufficient people, because they see no need for God. But those who have the slightest perception about the awesome greatness of God and the abject, desperate needs of man are drawn to prayer like a moth to a flame. They simply *must* pray. There is no other option. Only the infinite God can meet their needs and the needs of others.

Consistency in prayer is a wonderful thing. Redundancy is not. When I find myself praying the same things in the same words for the same people day after day, I know my prayer life has become stale. At those times I stop and ask a few questions: Do I have a sense of the presence of Christ? Am I enjoying the Lord? Is there freshness in my relationship with Him? Am I being honest about hurts, fear, or anger in my life? How much praise and thanksgiving is present in my devotions? What am I really depending on God to do in these situations?

Too many of us pray the same rote, shallow prayers day after day. Or we bring a grocery list of wants to God without seeking intimacy with Him. Or we don't pray at all. Prayer is not just a nice thing to do. It is a vital necessity for anyone who genuinely desires to honor Christ.

The recorded prayers of Paul show us the richness of his perception of God and his understanding of people. He was burdened and busy, yet he spent far more time in praise and thanksgiving than most Christians do. (We tend to get to the "I want" part of prayer very quickly.) Typically, Paul included three aspects in his prayers: thanksgiving, praise, and requests for wisdom and strength. (See Ephesians 1:15-23; Philippians 1:3-11; and Colossians 1:3-14.) Paul seemed to be in no hurry, as if prayer were of utmost importance to him.

Martin Luther had a similar view of his utter dependence on God and the necessity of prayer. He once said, "I have so much to do today, I shall have to spend half of it in prayer."

Evangelism, discipleship, and prayer are elements of a cutting-edge ministry, but two strong forces dull this cutting edge for most Christians. The first misdirected function is emphasis on a business model of ministry. The second errant force is dependence upon people instead of God (practical atheism).

Choosing to avoid an MBA style of ministry

Gordon McDonald, the former head of Intervarsity Christian Fellowship, has observed that for centuries the heroes of mankind were military men. But today our heroes are businessmen. Courageous battles for home and country have been replaced by hostile corporate takeover attempts, motivated by the thirst for profit. Audie Murphy has been replaced by T. Boone Pickens.

Subtly, an MBA mentality has crept into the church and parachurch organizations. A business model has begun to pervade the ministry. Criteria for decision making has become based on sound business principles instead of sound biblical principles. The cutting edge of prayer, evangelism, and discipleship has given way to the planning and execution of programs.

I always enjoy talking to my friend Robert McGee, the president of Rapha, a Christian counseling organization.

Though Robert uses sound business techniques and Rapha has grown phenomenally, he maintains a healthy, fresh perspective on the reality of the supernatural.

When I get bogged down in the philosophies and strategies of what makes an organization click, I am encouraged to hear Robert describing how the Lord directed him in the decisions on a particular problem. When I ask him a question, he does not rely on organizational planning for the solution. Instead, he asks me, "What does God want you to do?"

Recently, Robert was telling me about a significant advance for Rapha's ministry. Typically, he explained, "The Lord paved the way."

I replied, "He did? I thought it was your slick idea that got the job done."

"Well, Pat, who do you think gave me the idea?" Robert asked, and I realized I had been gently admonished. Robert is well aware that our struggle is not against flesh, blood, and organizational charts. Our struggle is primarily a spiritual battle that is waged in all kinds of arenas, including the boardroom.

Examples of this Christianized MBA phenomenon are legion. One leader essentially became a recluse because he was so involved in planning every detail. He expressed no concern for people under his leadership, and they felt they were being used to accomplish his goals. Another spent so much time coordinating programs that he seldom found time to talk to people about their personal needs or to share the Gospel with anyone. Others lose their emphasis on prayer, one-to-one evangelism, and discipleship. They put their time and effort into program planning and then expect the program to get results. But programs are only valid if they enhance—not replace—evangelism, discipleship, and prayer.

Recently I asked a busy pastor of a college ministry, "Do you spend time with your people?" He instantly answered, "Yes," but a follow-up question seemed to be in order.

"What do you do when you get together with them?"

"We go over their responsibilities for that week."

"Is that all?"

"Yes, there's no time for anything else."

It is sad when a pastor can't find time to do anything but administer and manage. Several factors stimulate this MBA mentality at the expense of biblical models of ministry.

1. The secular world pursues rewards and values success, prestige, and power. Compassion, humility, and servanthood are rarely valued or promoted.

2. It's not hard to find role models of successful business people, but there are few readily identifiable role models of those who humbly shepherd others.

3. Our society is becoming heavily dependent on fast-paced technology: computers, robots, videos, etc. Meaningful personal interaction is becoming rare.

4. It is easier to devise strategies, plans, tools, organizational charts, and perk sheets than to be vulnerable and compassionate. Plans and programs are easier to control and less threatening than people, who may not respond positively and may even disapprove of us.

5. It is easier to measure success with management techniques (numbers, charts, and graphs) than in terms of intangibles, such as spiritual growth.

6. It is more expedient to get rid of slow or disagreeable people than to take time to help them. We too often want to move with the movers and protect ourselves from people who need help with their problems.

7. Because our models are program orientated, we reward and promote those who are successful at running programs. This system is self-perpetuating.

Business techniques and computers are not inherently evil. The problem is letting such things become the standard for a Christian ministry. We can and should use planning and administration to enhance a biblical ministry of prayer, evangelism, and discipleship, but we should never allow business disciplines to replace spiritual ones. "Give to Caesar what is Caesar's, and to God what is God's" (Matthew 22:21, NIV).

Finding a proper balance is a matter of priority and degree. Attention given to planning and administration should strengthen ministry. For instance, leading a Sunday school class or Bible study group may allow you to establish deep relationships, share the Gospel, and organize a network of prayer.

Spending quality time with people means that time allotted to administration may need to be reduced. (But you may actually manage better when you are motivated by interaction with others.)

The management/ministry dilemma provides a constant tension for me. It is so easy to dive into my "to do list" instead of spending time with people. I like to see tangible, measurable results. (Isn't a check in a box tangible?) Evangelism, discipleship, and prayer take time, and they aren't very tangible. But God has called me to be a laborer in His harvest, not just to manage my "to do list."

The myth needs to be dispelled that prayer, evangelism, and discipleship must be rigorously planned in order to be effective. Certainly we need to establish biblical goals and plans, but if a person is enamored with the love of Christ and gripped with the needs of others, it is amazing how many spontaneous opportunities come up. We need to leave room for our inscrutable and loving God to use us in ways we cannot plan.

Is your ministry based on business principles or biblical principles? Here are some questions to ask yourself:

1. Do I relate to people with the same kind of affection as Jesus would? How do I respond when they fail?

2. Am I seeking to serve or to be recognized?

3. Do I spend more time in planning or in prayer?

4. When I succeed, do I show more appreciation for people and strategies than for Christ?

5. Am I committed to the intangibles of spiritual growth, or must my plans and goals be airtight?

6. Whom do I emulate? Who are my heroes?

7. Has God gifted me in the area of administration or in cutting-edge ministry? Which area am I pursuing?

8. What steps do I need to take from where I am now?

Choosing to avoid practical atheism

The harmful trend toward a business model for ministry is made worse by trusting ourselves. Far too many of us give lip service to God, but in reality we are practical atheists. Our selfish actions do nothing to indicate His influence on our lives. If our secret pursuit is to honor ourselves, then success, pleasure, and recognition make sense. Evangelism becomes secondary, prayer becomes optional, and discipleship becomes thoroughly man centered. We ask, "How will this relationship benefit me?" rather than "How can we honor the Lord together?"

Stephen Charnock poignantly addresses the issue of practical atheism in his epic work, *The Existence and Attributes of God* (Baker). To him, it is unthinkable to say that we believe in God if we don't conform our lives to His will:

We deny His sovereignty when we violate His laws. We disgrace His holiness when we cast our filth before His face. We disparage His wisdom when we set up another rule as the guide of our actions. We slight His sufficiency when we prefer a satisfaction in sin before happiness in Him alone, and His goodness when we judge it not strong enough to attract us to Him.

A couple of years ago, Joyce and I went with two other couples to a concert by a popular singer. I was struck by the enthusiasm and adoration of the crowd. They purchased T-shirts, albums, tapes, and posters. They clapped, stood, and cheered for one song after another. The majority of the people there would have said that they believed in God (according to Gallup Polls), yet I wondered how they would have responded if Jesus walked out on stage instead of the singer.

Charnock wrote:

Men gladly cheer idols other than God, and stand
with their ready obedience to serve them. They will
follow other things rather than cheer the heart of
God by their obedience and worship.

We pick and choose the attributes of God and the aspects of God's will that appeal to us. Then we "interpret" them so they justify the unfettered pursuit of selfish goals. We cannot say that God is loving and deny that God is just. We cannot say God wants me to have an abundant life and deny that God wants me to be obedient to Him no matter what. We should abandon the ludicrous notion that we can shape God and His will to suit our whims. He is, indeed, God! We are the ones who should be shaped by His awesome character and directed by His sovereign will.

Our shallow prayers and lack of compassion for people are reflections of practical atheism. Our thoughts and dreams indicate who we love most, honor most, and depend on most. The omnipotent God, the Creator of the vast expanse of the universe, became a man. He was rejected and murdered so we could escape eternal destruction and receive forgiveness and purpose, yet we have little appreciation for Him.

Our thoughts dwell on ourselves, and our dreams focus on the glories of tomorrow's triumphs, honors, and pleasures. As much as I study, speak, teach, and write about the priority of seeking after Christ and His kingdom, I am often embarrassed by how much I think about myself. "I wonder if I'll get that promotion." "People seemed to like that talk I gave last night." "That new shirt really looks good (or bad) on me." "What did she mean when she said that I'm 'kind of funny'?" "Can Catherine really see my bald spot from fifteen feet away?"

It is a real struggle to value unseen spiritual priorities more than the glitz of Hollywood or the approval of people. So many of the stimuli we receive every day center squarely on the pursuit of self. We must make a concerted effort to avoid being conformed to the world, and to fill our minds with thanksgiving, praise, and truth about God. Then our lives will be transformed so that we glorify the One who is worthy. The process is slow and may be painful, but it is most rewarding.

Man was not made as animals, plants, and other works to materially glorify God, but as a rational creature to intentionally honor God by obedience to His rule, dependence on His goodness, and zeal for His glory.

We need evangelists, disciplers, and shepherds. The biblical models are clear. People need answers, but they also need models who are honest about the real struggle in life. Seeing God work in people's lives is stimulating and encouraging, but it takes vulnerability, perception, and patience. Let us commit ourselves to a grass-roots ministry of prayer, evangelism, and discipleship—the cutting edge.

QUESTIONS

1. *Has anyone ever discipled you? What did he/she do? How did you respond?*

2. *What is the primary reason(s) you don't share the Gospel more than you do?*

3. *What would make your prayers more honoring to God?*

4. Spend some more time examining each of the questions on pages 192-193 concerning the MBA style of ministry. How can you improve in this area?

5. Are you a "practical atheist"? If so, what are some things you can do to focus more clearly on God?

6. Read Colossians 1:28, 29. What does this passage teach about a cutting-edge ministry? Do you fall short? What can you do about it? How can you incorporate this change into your schedule?

Chapter 16
Decisions in the Marketplace

It was a hot, beautiful day on the beach at Panama City, Florida. The sixty or so students held a series of tug-of-war contests during the afternoon, drawing a crowd of 250 to 300 to watch Georgians pull against Alabamians (my Georgia team lost every time), North pull against South, Auburn against Alabama, eight girls against three guys, and any other combination we could imagine. Some contestants were burly hulks; some were runts. Some were sober; some weren't.

After the tugs, Robbie announced on the megaphone, "We're with Campus Crusade for Christ, and we want to talk to people about how they can have a personal relationship with Jesus Christ." Soon dozens of two-, three-, or four-person groups were discussing Christ.

A couple of hours later, we trudged through the sand back to our hotel. We gathered around the pool and listened to exciting reports from the afternoon. Jeff and Kent had talked to two high school boys who trusted Christ. Annika and Kim talked for two hours to a girl from Ohio who was interested. Joe met some football players from Alabama who were more interested in themselves than in God. Kathy led the first person she talked with to Christ.

Though not everybody we talked to received Christ, virtually every person was glad to talk to us. We prayed, thanking God for His love and power, and that He had worked in so many lives that day. We prayed that those who had become Christians would grow in their faith (we would be meeting with most of them again the next day), and that those who didn't respond would understand the compelling grace of Christ. It had been a remarkable day of ministry.

But my enthusiasm was tempered a few weeks later. The local director for Campus Crusade for Christ had sponsored a reunion at a western university. About 40 people who had been involved in CCC during the past few years came to renew old acquaintances. A few of them were doing well spiritually, but most of them said that their involvement in college was the highlight of their Christian lives.

Their words hurt the director deeply. His desire had been to prepare them for a lifetime of service for the Lord, not just a flash-in-the-pan college experience.

What had happened? Why wasn't their college experience a springboard to greater maturity and broader service for Christ? Why do so many people consider their college years a pinnacle in Christian development?

College vs. "the real world"

As a friend said recently, the college campus and the real world marketplace are two different worlds. A person making the transition from one to the other needs to understand the fundamental differences: in environments, goals, benefits, and liabilities. If students aren't prepared to enter the secular marketplace, they risk becoming spiritual dropouts.

College students need to anticipate these characteristics and pressures so they can continue a personal relationship with God and a significant ministry after graduation. Those who have already made that difficult transition may need to make necessary corrections.

When you are seventy years old, what do you want to be able to say about your life? Many people recall with regret their pursuit of meaningless things. When I look back on my life, I want no regrets. I want to be able to say with the apostle Paul, "I have fought the good fight, I have finished the course, I have kept the faith" (II Timothy 4:7).

The opportunities to represent Christ in the marketplace are almost inexhaustible, but sometimes you _do_ have to look for them. The youthful feeling of immortality, self-centeredness, and self-sufficiency may blind people to their need for Christ in college. But when the reality of marital problems, family conflicts, and financial pressures overpowers them, they often cry out for help. They are ready for someone to tell them about God's love, forgiveness, power, wisdom, and strength.

Wonderful opportunities for ministry are created during the move from the campus to the marketplace. Let's examine the contrasts between college and career in preparation to help those who may need it.

College and university campuses are quite homogeneous. Everybody is about the same age, with similar goals and the same sets of classes. The marketplace is heterogeneous. There are wide varieties of careers, living conditions, life-styles, goals, salaries, and age-groups.

The campus environment is sheltered, sealed off from the rest of the world. This separation incubates young minds, but it often prevents the failures and diverse circumstances that build strong convictions. The marketplace is an open system. There is a vast array of influences and opportunities for both success and failure.

While in college, a person is considered a "young person." Someone in the marketplace, whether 18 or 88, is considered an adult and is treated as such.

Finances for those in college are provided by one or a combination of sources: grants, scholarships, loans, parental support, and part-time jobs. In the marketplace, a person's income is based almost exclusively on personal productivity—how well he performs on the job.

A college student's parents usually express a lot of care and concern. In the marketplace, the parental role diminishes, especially as one gets married and has a family. The primary authority becomes the boss, who is usually more interested in corporate profits than in the well-being of the employee. (One businessman recently noted that current interest in business journals about the well-being of employees is not based on compassion at all. It's just good business because happy workers are more productive. "Caring for employees" is just another way to fatten the bottom line.)

College students tend to have a simple life-style. They are usually able to do what they want to do when they want to do it. In the marketplace, the complexity of life accelerates rapidly as responsibilities increase. People get married, have children, get promotions, get laid off, make mortgage payments, care for elderly parents, and deal with their own physical problems. Spontaneity and personal freedom are limited.

The goal of the college is to prepare students for the marketplace through intellectual stimulation and professional/technical development. The goal of the marketplace is profit. Efficiency becomes of foremost importance.

On campus, religion and ethics are openly discussed in virtually every arena. In the marketplace, most employers resent employees using company time to talk about God. That, they insist, should be done on your own time. In some companies, an open witness for Christ is grounds for dismissal.

The relatively flexible schedules of college students allow them to team up with others to share their faith or encourage other Christians. The Christian in the marketplace often must minister alone, making use of the limited time he has available. Going it alone takes considerably more courage and stamina than it does to minister with group support.

Evangelistic contacts are easy to make on campus. Opportunities arise through dorm questionnaires, talks to Greek houses, large evangelistic meetings, and of course, with friends and classmates. Many professors will allow Christians to take a survey of the class and follow up with those who are interested. One can't go up and down the hall of a law office or corporate headquarters and pass out surveys. The audience is more restricted (usually 10 to 30 people), and since there is daily contact, a more personal, less confrontational approach is needed to begin a conversation about Christ.

Many campus activities stimulate spiritual growth: conferences, retreats, Bible studies, singing groups, prayer meetings, and so forth. There may be so many activities that students float from event to event without time to reflect and internalize biblical convictions. A decrease in available time and increase in responsibilities leave less time for activities in the marketplace. A person must be motivated to introduce others to Christ, and he must be the master of his personal schedule to make his limited amount of time as effective as possible.

Added pressures in the marketplace

The previous compendium of observations is not 100% true in any given situation. However, it gives basic characteristics of the vastly differing worlds of the college campus and the marketplace. Christians in the marketplace certainly face a number of pressure points.

The vast majority of Christians who enter the business and professional world are driven by the same purpose as their

non-Christian colleagues: success, comfort, and approval.
Career advancement, personal improvement, and fun form the
criteria for decision making. If there was a flickering desire to
serve Christ and pursue personal goals, Christian service is
usually quickly overwhelmed by the time and attention given
to personal achievement. Expedience and comfort preclude
godliness and compassion.

Most people have financial problems, and Christians are
no exception. A typical college graduate thinks a $30,000 an-
nual salary will be wonderful. But the problem is not how much
people make—it is how much they spend. American families
today spend more than they make, and consumer debt in this
country is staggering.

A student who is graduating often has friends who have
been working for a couple of years and who are driving BMW's.
They go skiing twice a year and make several trips to the
beach. The student surmises, "Why can't I have all this, too?"
And the bank says, "Indeed, why not? Here's a credit card and
a loan application for your new car. Enjoy!" Four years of pent-
up desire and the high expectations of landing a lucrative job
make for a ravenous consumer.

Many young couples I know experience the devastating
treadmill of twin financial evils: (1) acquiring too much and
inevitably finding themselves unable to pay creditors, and (2)
spending an enormous amount of time and emotional energy to
get out of debt. Too much debt and too little time robs the
couple (and their children) of the stability they need to focus
on the Lord, to strengthen family ties, and to reach out to
others. Debt often triggers self-centeredness and bitterness.

Postponing spiritual commitment

Before choosing a company, find out about the unwritten
expectations regarding time and loyalty. A good friend recently
changed jobs. He told me about the company for which he had

been working. He said, "Those people expected me to give my life for the company. The pressure was unbelievable!" Early mornings, late nights, weekends, and unexpected phone calls at home from the boss all took their toll. His boss fully expected him to put the company first and his family second. (His ministry had no chance at all.)

Some young executives look at the demanding 60-to-70-hour-per-week work load and decide, "I'll become a success so other people will respect me and listen to me. When I'm a vice president, I'll take time for a ministry." It's a nice theory, but it almost never happens. Why? Because when someone gives disproportionate amounts of time and attention to a career, zeal for the Lord atrophies and ministry skills become rusty. Even if he does make it to vice president, he is usually little more than a nice Christian businessman who has lost his cutting-edge love for Christ and his concern for others.

Try to get an honest salary for an honest day's work, but don't let the company own you. You can only have one Lord. Don't let it be your boss at work.

Most college seniors feel very comfortable with their station in life. They are the elite on campus. They know the ropes. They typically find it easy to take the initiative socially, academically, and if they are Christians, spiritually.

But a strange and sudden metamorphosis takes place. These tigers turn into frightened kittens the first day on the job. The student who was so confident with old friends, classes, and expectations now has an entirely new environment. He or she must cope with a new job, new people who aren't friends yet (and who may not *become* friends), and a new living situation, among other things. The new kid on the job faces the significant and constant risk of failure and rejection. The primary goal becomes to minimize the risk.

For most Christians entering the marketplace, the risk of failure and rejection is quite beyond their ability to cope. They quickly get sucked into climbing the ladder, acquiring the right stuff, and saying the right things to please others because they have not developed strong biblical convictions.

Consequently, the risks of living for God in the marketplace are too much for them. They are already "risked out." They can't handle the prospect of additional failure and rejection. They pursue escape and conformity instead.

The recognition of these fears is a good first step. This realization should lead to a reexamination of our position in Christ: we are deeply loved, completely forgiven, and totally accepted because Christ's death paid for our sins. He has given us life, hope, and purpose so that we don't have to succumb to the fear of failure and rejection.

Yet even the realization of these truths isn't enough. We need the affirming, vulnerable, supportive environment of a few Christian friends to help us assimilate and apply the truths of God's Word. We need these people to encourage us when we take steps of faith, and we need them to comfort us when we fail.

Henry's experience

Henry worked hard, but he never thought he did enough for the company. He always felt his boss expected more of him. He also thought his wife, children, friends, and the people at church expected more of him. He was consumed with the desire to prove to these people that he was OK, but no matter how well he did (and he usually did quite well), it never seemed to be enough.

Then Henry began to understand that Christ's unconditional love and acceptance was the answer to his insecurities. As we talked the other day, he told me, "Pat, I can't tell you what a difference it has made in my life! I don't struggle much with the fears of rejection and failure anymore. What a relief!" A few minutes later he was telling me about how his security in

Christ had allowed him to begin discipling a group of men. He is giving more and more of his time to this group because he's no longer afraid of the disapproval of others.

Initiative for a cutting-edge ministry of prayer, evangelism, and discipleship comes from a heart that is on rock-solid ground—secure in Jesus. Fear is the mud that bogs us down and keeps our focus on our own problems.

The solutions to our problems are usually multifaceted. We need to begin the painful process of being honest about our fears. We need others to provide warmth and stimulation so our faith will grow. And we need the Holy Spirit to give us wisdom and strength. In such an environment we can develop a tenacious commitment to live by the love, forgiveness, and power of Christ.

Try to establish such a commitment before you enter the marketplace. But if you are already there, it is never too late to develop these convictions and to begin to use the criterion of "What will honor Christ the most?" Do whatever it takes to truly live for Jesus. Steps of correction may be difficult, but they will be well worth it when you give an account of your life to the One who said, "To whom much is given, much is required."

The goal is to finish well, not just to get off to a good start. Be alert to the insidious pressures and pitfalls around you. Some are obviously wrong (such as immorality and unethical business practices) and relatively easy to spot. Others are less obvious, yet hinder your effectiveness for Christ.

You must be alert to avoid the gnawing temptations to have what everybody else has and do whatever everybody else is doing. Jesus warned, "The thief [Satan] comes to steal, and to kill, and destroy" (John 10:10). Peter cautions us, "Be on the alert. Your adversary, the devil, prowls about like a roaring lion, seeking someone to devour" (I Peter 5:8). Satan doesn't play games. He fully intends to cripple you so you can't represent Christ in a world that so desperately needs Him.

Jesus warned against self-glory when He rebuked the
Pharisees: "You are those who justify yourselves in the sight of
men, but God knows your hearts; for that which is highly
esteemed among men is detestable in the sight of God" (Luke
16:15). What is highly esteemed at your office and among your
friends? Do you find yourself esteeming those things, too?

A need for encouragement and accountability

It helps when other Christians encourage us and hold us
accountable. I meet with a group of businessmen every week for
prayer and Bible study. We derive great strength from each
other's understanding, accountability, and encouragement. Yet
each of us has made the decision that even if no one else follows Christ, we will go it alone. We benefit from each other,
but we are not totally dependent on each other. That individ-
ual commitment makes our relationships more Christ-centered
and wholesome than if we had parasitic relationships with each
other. And each person in the group has committed himself to
evangelism, discipleship, and prayer.

To live a radical life for Christ in a self-centered world is
not easy. It takes the strength and wisdom that only God's
Word and God's Spirit can provide. It also takes guts, persistence, and encouragement along the way.

QUESTIONS

For Students:

1. *How sheltered are you? How do you know?*

2. *When you daydream about graduating and entering
   the marketplace, what do you think about?*

3. *What would you like to be true of you in each of the
   following areas:*

Wrong goals—

Shallow convictions about godliness and ministry—

Debt—

Corporate expectations—

The need for initiative—

4. *What specific steps do you need to take to see these convictions (in #3) become reality? Which one will be first? When?*

For Those in the Marketplace:

1. *Which contrast(s) were you most surprised to discover when you made the transition to the marketplace? How did it affect you?*

2. *Examine each of the following pressure points and honestly evaluate how you're doing:*

Wrong goals—

Shallow convictions about godliness and ministry—

Debt—

Corporate expectations—

The need for initiative—

3. *What would you like to be true of you in each area?*

4. *What steps do you need to take? Which one first? When? How?*

Chapter 17
Facing Inevitable Spiritual Warfare

When a person chooses to give God top priority, he or she will inevitably notice changes taking place in attitudes and life-style. Motives change from "have to" to "want to." A new intimacy with the Lord becomes evident. God's Spirit overflows into the person's words, thoughts, behavior, and activities. And decisions are made with greater confidence, based firmly on a sense of purpose.

These benefits are all evidence of the work of God. But there is another piece of evidence that is just as much a part of a person's new desire to honor the Lord: spiritual warfare.

It's nice to know that God notices our renewed commitment to Him and rewards it accordingly. Yet our desire to honor God does not go unnoticed in other areas of the spiritual realm, where forces are eager to have us fail. The world system, our fallen nature, and Satan all threaten to squash any desire for renewal. Let's examine some of the problems and the solutions in this warfare.

Emotional Wounds

Emotional pain is a product of our fallen nature. Sinful-
ness causes the love and unity that God desires for relationships
to turn into bitterness, hurt, and depression. The family and
the body of Christ were designed to provide strong nurturing
environments so people can experience God's love and power,
but these institutions are facing a 50 percent divorce rate,
alarming rises in alcoholism and drug abuse, and many other
threats to the family structure. Sadly, statistics for the church
are not far behind the national averages.

These broad statistics are made up of many individuals
who have been affected by instability. People from dysfunctional families (including the whole spectrum from severe to mild)
learn to deny their feelings because they aren't allowed to feel
and express pain within the family. They either learn that they
can't trust anybody, or that they have to trust everybody, even
the untrustworthy. They learn to perceive other people and
situations through the distorted lenses of their dysfunctional
families. Manipulation, lying, hatred, compulsion, and passivity
are just parts of a normal life, or so they believe.

Pain, anger, and depression can run deep, even in the
lives of sincere Christians, but there is often severe pressure to
deny the reality of these wounds. We want to think we're OK,
and we want others to believe we're doing fine, so we try to
struggle along.

Since the emotional, relational, intellectual, and spiritual aspects of our lives are all woven together, Satan and his
forces can use our pain against us. He can reinforce negative
perceptions about God, suggesting that God doesn't love us,
that He is harsh and condemning, or that He is only using us.
Our inability to be honest about our own hurt and anger makes
forgiveness much more difficult, and the powers of darkness
oppress us in these areas too. (See Ephesians 4:26-27 and
Matthew 18:21-35.)

We can develop powerful defense mechanisms of denial, withdrawal, and drivenness to block this pain and win approval. We can read and teach about God's love and forgiveness, yet continue to live in guilt, self-condemnation, and even self-hatred. That's why this book contains several chapters about our security and significance as children of God.

People with a solid emotional foundation can take the truths of Scripture and run with them. Struggles and conflicts are a part of everyone's life, yet most people seem to progress fairly well. But those who are wounded emotionally, spiritually, and relationally need to be realistic about their progress. It will come, but they need to be able to walk before they can run.

A man who has been chained to a prison wall for years may dream of running, but he can't even move freely about his cell. When he is freed, he still may dream of running, but his steps will be a faltering few. Slowly, as his strength returns he can walk. After months or years of patience and increased strength, he can begin to jog. His progress is slow, yet realistic for his condition. In the same way, we need to be patient and realistic about emotional, relational, and spiritual restoration. Though we may dream of running, we first must learn to walk.

It is easy to see how an emotionally wounded, passive person fits this illustration. But ironically, it may be that compulsive, driven people who seem to be running well are just as imprisoned. They sprint not out of health, but as a defense mechanism to meet their emotional needs. They too need to be freed and strengthened in a patient, honest, and affirming environment. Emotional wounds are a major hindrance to the development of many of us, but honesty, love, and patience can provide healing and strength.

Removing all traces of sin

The more we experience the depth of Christ's forgiveness, and the more we become aware of sin's tragic effects on

ourselves and others, the more we will want to respond deci-
sively. Jesus instructed:

> If your right eye causes you to sin, gouge it out and
> throw it away. It is better for you to lose one part of
> your body than for your whole body to be thrown into
> hell. And if your right hand causes you to sin, cut it
> off and throw it away. It is better for you to lose one
> part of your body than for your whole body to go into
> hell (Matthew 5:29, 30, *NIV*).

The story of Thomas Cranmer illustrates this aversion to
sin and deciding to deal ruthlessly with it. Cranmer was a brilliant man who lived the quiet life of a scholar at Oxford University in the early sixteenth century. When he was thirty years
old, he read the teaching of Martin Luther and gave up other
academic pursuits so he could devote all his time to the study of
Reformation theology.

The summer of 1529 brought high drama to England.
Henry VIII was searching for a way to divorce his queen,
Catherine of Aragon. Quite by chance, Cranmer discussed the
issues surrounding the proposed divorce with two men of King
Henry's court. The men were surprised and delighted to hear
his suggestion: Let churchmen in England, not Rome, decide if
the divorce was legal. The two men hurried to tell the king.
Henry thought Cranmer's idea was brilliant.

Soon, King Henry split with the church in Rome and
established the Church of England. Under the new jurisdiction, the divorce proceeded predictably without any problems.
The thankful Henry appointed Cranmer the Archbishop of
Canterbury—head of the Church of England. The scholarly
and reclusive Cranmer, however, didn't want the public
position. He delayed the short trip to London for seven weeks,
hoping that King Henry would forget about him. Henry didn't.

After a few years, another upheaval followed as Queen
Mary took the throne after Henry and restored Catholicism as

the state religion. As the daughter of the deposed Catherine of Aragon, Mary understandably despised Thomas Cranmer for his role in her mother's divorce. In 1552, she had Cranmer arrested for heresy.

After languishing in jail for three years, Cranmer's bitter trial began on September 12, 1555. His stalwart spirit began to fade. Worn down by three years in prison, unrelenting legal arguments, importunities of well-meaning friends, and subtle suggestions of guileful enemies, Cranmer gave in. The friars and doctors wrote out a recantation, and he signed it.

He had been promised freedom and the restoration of his dignities if he would recant, but the vengeful queen still insisted that Cranmer be put to death. The rigors of his imprisonment had been severe, but his emotional torment was unbearable. For the promise of freedom he had denied the Lord, yet still he would be burned at the stake.

On March 21, 1556, Cranmer was greeted, without warning, by his executioners. A prepared text, affirming his allegiance to the Pope, was given to him to be read at the final hearing. But he secretly wrote another document and carried the substitute with him.

As Cranmer rose to speak for the last time, the people were shocked as he recanted his recantation and affirmed his allegiance to Christ and the Scriptures. At the close of his statement, he held out the hand he had previously used to sign the document of recantation, and he said, "With this hand I denied my Lord. It shall be burned first."

"Madness!" screamed some. Others tried to argue with him as he was escorted to the stake, but Cranmer paid no attention. He only stopped to say good-bye to a few friends.

He was stripped to his shirt, an iron chain was tied around him, and the fire was set. As it burned close to him, he stretched out his right hand into the flame, holding it steady and immovable. The hand burned completely off before his

body began to burn. Then he stood steadfast with his eyes lifted
to heaven, often repeating "This unworthy right hand," and
"Lord Jesus, receive my spirit." After about forty-five minutes
in the flames, Cranmer died.

As painful and disagreeable as it may be, we must identify our specific pursuits for self-glory so we can deal with them
specifically and ruthlessly. These pursuits rob us of love for God
and render us ineffective for His service. They defame the One
who died for us and bought us.

> Do you not know that your body is a temple of the
> Holy Spirit who is in you, whom you have from God,
> and that you are not your own? For you have been
> bought with a price: Therefore, glorify God in your
> body (I Corinthians 6:19, 20).

Sin needs to be acknowledged and reproved in brutal
honesty, but there are less sinister activities and attitudes which
also hinder obedience to Christ. The writer to the Hebrews
exhorts us to "lay aside every encumbrance . . . and let us run
with endurance the race that is set before us, fixing our eyes on
Jesus" (Hebrews 12:1, 2).

A runner may be able to run while he wears an overcoat
and carries an anvil, but he won't win. Similarly, we become
weighed down and encumbered when we possess too much or
too little of a good thing. We need to critically analyze even
the good things we do to see if we are hindered at all by them.
Then we can deal with them ruthlessly.

Choosing the right biblical priorities

Most of us want the best of both worlds: success and
pleasure, and the joy and peace of being a Christian. But this
syncretism is detestable to God. He deserves unqualified loyalty
and obedience. After all, He is the Lord. That depth of commitment is our only reasonable response because He is worthy
of our love and obedience. If we search for biblical priorities

without intending to obey, we are deluding ourselves and wasting our time. The willingness to obey is a prerequisite to learning truth (John 7:17).

We also need discernment to detect our culture's demand for instant everything. We are accustomed to fast food, fast banking, fast sex, and fast solutions to any problem. I can jump into my car, zip over to an instant teller to get some cash, fill up with self-serve gas (not enough time to check the oil today), and pull through McDonald's drive-in window to grab a value-pack combo lunch. Then I rush back to the office where I expect to solve every problem with a ten-minute phone call. (Really big problems take fifteen minutes.)

But the inscrutable, omniscient God is not worked so easily into our timetables. We go against the grain of culture when we choose to pursue spiritual goals which are eternal and invisible instead of instant, visible goals.

The hectic pace and complexity of our culture lead to shallowness if we aren't careful. We need to have time alone— time to read, study, and reflect. We cannot choose to live by biblical goals and priorities if we do not know them, and we cannot know them if we don't study the Scriptures seriously.

Perhaps this book and others will increase your understanding of biblical priorities, but be wary of processed truth. Study the Scriptures yourself.

Many excellent Bible study methods and tools are available for those interested in getting started. A friend of mine showed me a method years ago that is both simple and profound. It is based on II Timothy 3:16, 17 (*NIV*):

All Scripture is God-breathed and is useful for teaching, rebuking, correcting and training in righteousness, so that the man of God may be thoroughly equipped for every good work.

Select a book of Scripture. (You might want to consider Romans.) First read it at one sitting. Then read through it several times. Then study one paragraph at a time by answering these questions:

1. What does the passage teach me? (Teaching)

2. Do I fall short? (Reproof)

3. What am I going to do about it? (Correction)

4. How will I work it into my schedule? (Training in righteousness)

I have used this method for many years, and it has helped me apply truth from God's Word. The strength of this method is application—putting shoe leather to Bible study.

About a year ago, I began an intriguing study of radical passages in the Gospels. These four books are peppered with poignant passages, but I had never looked at them together. These passages are listed at the back of this book in Appendix B. You may want to select one or two passages a day to study using the previous method. It has been very stimulating and encouraging to me, and I hope you will benefit from it as well.

Our priorities are determined by our purpose in life, which raises a number of questions: Are our interests temporal or eternal? Do we want to be free to make our own choices? How does an understanding of the Scriptures help us serve God gladly? How grateful are we that Jesus has rescued us from eternal condemnation, hopelessness, despair, and emptiness? To what extent do we allow Him to give us life and hope?

We determine our priorities by asking, "Do I want to please Christ?" and if so, "How can I please Christ?" Such is the essence of sincere and pure devotion to Christ.

Choosing productive activities

When we make a genuine attempt to reorient priorities, we will realize that much of our time is spent in activities that conflict with our purpose of honoring Christ and our desire to live by biblical values. Working sixty to seventy hours a week, watching hour after hour of television, or being involved in questionable ethical and moral incidents must be reevaluated. That time can be used to develop our relationships with the Lord, our families, and others; to pray, study, and reflect on the Scriptures; or in a myriad of other ways that honor the Lord.

Sadly, most of us see the problem, but we take only small, incremental steps. We seldom go far enough to effect significant change. This Band-Aid approach is rarely successful. Radical surgery is often needed.

Tom is a friend who decided to take drastic action. He relates his experience: "I was praying for deeper fellowship with God, but my affections for Him were blocked by an attachment to possessions. I had a lust for knowledge and an unholy attachment to things. God didn't let me rest until there was a physical removal of the things on which I centered my affections."

Tom felt that the Lord wanted him to get rid of some favorite possessions. He had a missionary friend who needed money, so Tom sold his deer rifle, 12-gauge shotgun, jewelry, some of his clothes, and virtually all of his books and cassette tapes. He gave the money to his friend. Tom was left with only the Scriptures and a few clothes.

A few days later, Tom turned the page on his calendar to the next month. The caption was a quote from C. S. Lewis: "Behold, there is nothing now between us and Him." Tom sensed that this was God's confirmation of his overt and radical actions.

Tom's radical action of stripping away possessions was difficult, but it was a freeing experience for him. A different kind of radical action is seeking to influence others for Christ.

Wendel is a credit analyst at a large bank. His workload is demanding, but Wendel carves out time for his ministry. He would much rather talk about the men in his discipleship group than cash flow and net worth.

The six of them meet together each week. Wendel also meets with each of them individually to help them to share their faith with others. These men are catching Wendel's infectious enthusiasm. When he can't go with them, they pair up with each other to tell people about Christ. And these men are applying what they learn. Each has his own discipleship group. In all, there are forty men in this discipleship chain who are learning biblical priorities and putting them into practice.

"What can only one person accomplish?" someone has asked, as if looking for an excuse to do nothing. The answer is that one person can take the initiative to eliminate personal hindrances, and then make an impact for Christ. There is no greater fulfillment and no greater joy than seeing men and women respond to Christ.

Choosing productive habits

An instant solution often comes to an instant end. Shortcuts seem appealing, but the more painful and methodical discipline of cultivating habits is more realistic, effective, and long-lasting. When commitments are made, tomorrow's results are not as important as next month's and next year's. Time is a true test of commitment.

It has been estimated that it is seven times more difficult to change a habit than to establish one correctly at the outset. That fact is not meant to discourage you, but to give you perspective and tenacity. For those of us who have allowed success, pleasure, and prestige to determine our schedules and budgets, it will take a plan, discipline, and guts to bring about change for the glory of God. The transition may be awkward, but it is necessary.

Taking risks for Christ's sake is a habit that runs counter to our culture. There are many opportunists in our world who take great risks every day, but for themselves rather than for Christ.

What would be a "risky" thing for you to do for Christ? Talk to a neighbor about your relationship with Jesus? Tell your boss you can't work Saturday because you want to spend the day with your children? Ask a few friends to be in a Bible study group? Pray out loud with your roommate or spouse?

When you finally decide to live wholeheartedly for Christ, you don't have to make reservations on a ship to Outer Slobovia to be a missionary. But you *do* need to take a decisive first step.

Maybe you've already taken the first step. What's the next step for you? Paul Eschelman, director of "The Jesus Project" for Campus Crusade, said, "The best way to disciple somebody is to do something that scares you both!" What scares you?

Developing godly habits involves taking risks. The mood and intent of our culture says it's OK to be a nice Christian who doesn't ruffle any feathers. But if you aren't ruffling any feathers, it's because you're blending in too much. You can never be light and salt by blending in.

Be willing to accept the fact that some people will disapprove, even if you are very gracious in your stand for Christ. Think of how they disapproved of Christ Himself! But take the risks! Take the next step!

Theodore Roosevelt said, "Far better it is to dare mighty things, to win glorious triumphs even though checkered by failures, than to rank with those poor spirits who neither enjoy much nor suffer much, because they live in the gray twilight that knows not victory or defeat."

Choosing to withstand conflict

We will certainly receive opposition as we take a definitive stand for Christ. But we will also experience conflict if we refuse to honor Christ, so it is wise to experience hassles for good instead of ill. Conflict comes in a variety of ways, all designed to thwart us in our determination to honor Christ. Rejection by family members and peers, inconvenience, persecution by co-workers or neighbors, and Satan's continued deception can seem overwhelming at times. These challenges are even more overwhelming when we are caught unaware, not expecting the conflict.

We're often on the wrong battlefield fighting the wrong battles. Too often, our questions would sound like this if they were clearly stated:

How can I make enough money to have what I want and still give enough away so I won't feel guilty?

How can I move up the corporate and social ladders and still be a good Christian, too?

How can I do what my friends do so they will accept me, and still not feel too bad about myself?

We want our spiritual warfare to be like the armies of the sixteenth century who formed neat rows of soldiers on an open battlefield. But in actuality, it is much more like the battle of Iwo Jima in World War II. American forces were slowly and painfully gaining ground on the Japanese Empire. Fierce island fighting had brought us within bomber range of Tokyo, but an advanced base was needed for fighter escorts. General Douglas MacArthur decided that the tiny island of Iwo Jima would serve that purpose. Though it was only eight square miles, the Japanese had built a base from which their fighters harassed American shipping and intercepted American bombers on their bombing runs to Tokyo. The island had to be taken. Preparations were begun.

The Japanese recognized the strategic importance of Iwo Jima, so General Tadamichi Kuribayashi began preparing elaborate defenses. By the time the Americans invaded, General Kuribayashi had developed a network of excavated caves, well concealed and connected by deep tunnels. His aim was simply to hold out as long as possible, expecting no additional reinforcements because of America's naval and air superiority. He relied on the sheer defensive strength of his position, eschewing costly and characteristic Japanese counterattacks. The Japanese had 750 large guns, rocket launchers, mortars, and pillboxes, armed by twenty-one thousand men.

Supported by eight hundred ships, the eighty thousand American troops watched as a three-day air and naval bombardment pummeled the little island. Surely no one could live through such an offensive! But the Japanese sat deep in their tunnels and waited.

The Japanese soldiers had a total commitment to the Emperor. They considered it glorious to die for him. They were fierce and tenacious fighters.

When the Americans landed, they expected a cakewalk. They established a beachhead, but they were quickly pinned down by fire from the Japanese. After a day, they broke out and advanced, but the Japanese would pop up from one tunnel and fire. Then as the Americans concentrated on that hole, the Japanese would emerge from another hole behind them, mowing down the unsuspecting GIs. American casualties at Iwo Jima were among the worst in U. S. history. There were twenty-five thousand American casualties by the time the last stronghold was destroyed.

Iwo Jima was a testimony to Japanese courage and tenacity. Only 1,083 of their soldiers were captured by the Americans. The other twenty thousand were killed.

The spiritual forces of darkness are like the Japanese in the tunnels: treacherous and subtle. Just as the bombardment had little effect and the Americans were forced to resort to hand-to-hand combat, our battles cannot be won by a sermon a week. We need specific biblical truth to undergird specific biblical values as we engage in hand-to-hand spiritual combat day after day. Deception is not obvious, but it is deadly.

Christ, however, is far greater. His power is "far above all rule and authority and power and dominion, and every name that is named, not only in this age, but also in the one to come" (Ephesians 1:21).

What is spiritual warfare like? Do demons lurk behind every tree? Well, demons do indeed exist (though not behind trees) and they are active—more obviously in undeveloped countries than in the sophisticated western culture. But in the west, the covert activities of Satan and his minions are devastating. Their chief weapons are pride, lust, and discouragement.

I am especially vulnerable to discouragement. When I have failed, or even if it only seems that I have failed, I can easily feel defeated.

Recently, a paper I was working on had run into obstacle after obstacle. I thought it was good, but the reception it received was, shall we say, cool. At first I buckled down and tried to iron out the problems, but I guess my iron was cool, too. The problems just wouldn't go away. After a while, my zeal began to wane and I became disheartened.

I was reminded to persevere. The command in Joshua 1:9 helped me resolve to fight back against discouragement:

Have I not commanded you? Be strong and courageous! Do not tremble or be dismayed, for the Lord your God is with you wherever you go.

A raw recruit may have delusions about not getting his uniform dirty in battle, but a combat veteran expects to get dirty and sometimes bloodied. Our battle to honor Christ in every circumstance requires acute desire, persistence, and level-headed choices in the midst of life's firefights. We may receive a lot of encouragement from time to time, but there will always be times when we have hard, lonely choices to make. We can't please everybody. We dare not indulge in the luxury of trying to please ourselves. There is only One worthy of our total intensity, courage, and commitment.

As Paul instructed Timothy,

Endure hardship with us like a good soldier of
Christ Jesus. No one serving as a soldier gets involved
in civilian affairs—he wants to please his command-
ing officer (II Timothy 2:3, 4, *NIV*).

We can't deny that we are in a battle. It's real. We need
to acknowledge it and fight—so that Christ receives honor and
glory, and so that we don't get shot down.

Choosing to serve willingly

The focus on self-improvement, personal advancement,
and comfort robs us of appreciation for God and leaves us
apathetic to the pain of others. Our preoccupation with technology does little to develop us emotionally. (Have you ever
seen a computer with compassion?)

Television and movies numb our senses. We see thousands of murders and countless incidents of adultery, beatings,
divorce, and lust ("and now this message from Fluffy Fabric
Softener"). Instead of being horrified by such violence and lust,
we yawn and look for something a little more graphic. And
many of us become even more withdrawn and emotionally
sterile.

As we return to the roots of our faith and realize again
how awesome the infinite God is, and as we remember that,
though we were destined for hell, we have been rescued by His
strong love, then we will delight in expressing our unrestrained
love for the Lord. We will take time to behold the delightful-
ness of the Lord instead of hurrying from activity to activity.
And we will reflect with the psalmist:

Whom have I in heaven but you? And earth has
nothing I desire besides You. But as for me, it is good
to be near God. I have made the Sovereign Lord my
refuge; I will tell of all Your deeds (Psalm 73:25, 28,
NIV).

The genuine experience of the love of Christ always results in service. The more we realize that our deepest needs have been met by Christ's love and acceptance, the more we will be free to take our attention off ourselves and serve Him by helping others. The apostle Paul exemplified this selfless commitment to serve Christ. As he spoke for the last time with the leaders of the church in Ephesus, he told them:

> Compelled by the Spirit, I am going to Jerusalem, not knowing what will happen to me there. I only know that in every city the Holy Spirit warns me that prison and hardships are facing me. However, I consider my life worth nothing to me, if only I may finish the race and complete the task the Lord Jesus has given me—the task of testifying to the Gospel of God's grace (Acts 20:22-24, NIV).

That is the heart of humble Christian service: "I consider my life worth nothing to me." Those who are gripped with the greatness and love of Christ do not seek greatness for themselves. They do not care if they receive praise and promotion. They care only that Jesus is honored.

Several young women in our church wanted to be discipled, but they couldn't find anyone to lead them. "I'd love to, but I'm too busy," was the usual reply. Then they asked Barbara to consider leading them. She was busy too, with a family, a fellowship group, and other church responsibilities. Her choice was, in her words, "between ease and effort." The discipleship group would take some of her little remaining free time, but she said, "Somebody needs to lead these women. Why not me?" These women appreciate Barbara's humble, servant spirit and the fact that she made the choice to help them.

Some of us are driven by the pressure to succeed and be approved by others. This hyperactivity is not a virtue. These people have a very difficult time saying no because they don't want to risk someone being disappointed in them.

The alternative escape from the fear of failure and the fear of rejection is lethargy. Some people believe that if they don't try, they won't fail. That may be true, but neither will they succeed. Both hyperactivity and lethargy are methods to cope with emotional wounds or wrong goals. And both will prevent us from experiencing victory in our spiritual warfare.

When our goal becomes to honor Christ, we become less dependent on our success and others' approval for our security. We will develop selective intensity—focusing on the right things based on biblical values.

The only reasonable response to Christ is to strip away anything that hinders our effectiveness for Him. It is to take risks, to make radical choices, and to keep making those choices as we develop habits of godliness. Ultimately, our response is to live in reckless abandonment to Christ in passion and service—no matter what the cost, no matter what anyone might think. It is to live with a sincere and pure devotion to Christ.

QUESTIONS

1. *Describe your home environment or other relationships that have significantly shaped your life emotionally, relationally, and spiritually. What strengths have you developed? What hurts have you experienced? How do these affect your spiritual and emotional progress? What are realistic expectations for your progress? What factors would help you?*

2. *What sins or hindrances are tangling you up and slowing you down? How will you eliminate them from your life?*

3. *What would be a realistic goal for your personal study of the Scripture? When? Where? How?*

4. What are some possible steps of faith? What's the next step for you? What do you believe God wants you to do, even though it scares you?

5. What habit do you most need to establish in your life?

6. How can you identify spiritual warfare? What are some practical ways to prepare for it?

7. Do you think most Christians are relatively passionless today? Why or why not?

8. How are you serving Christ? How could you serve Him more?

9. Read Matthew 5:29, 30. Is Christ's statement exaggerated? Why or why not? Describe the level of your aversion to sin. Read Matthew 6:1-24. Where is your treasure? How can you tell?

Appendix A:

Choosing or Rechoosing A Vocation: Which Part Of the Harvest?

We called to "walk in a manner worthy of the Lord, to please Him in all respects" (Colossians 1:10). This call goes out to all of us, whether our vocational choice is Christian or secular. God uses some of His people in "full-time" Christian service and others as salt and light in a secular environment. Our response to this call is one of the most important choices we will ever make, so it seems appropriate to conclude this book with a discussion of this essential issue.

Many people will urge someone in transition (out of college, out of the military, or in mid-life) to consider "full-time Christian service." At such times, people seem to be asking, *What should I do for the rest of my life?* But the term "full-time Christian service" is a misnomer because each of us is called to serve Christ full time. The Scriptures indicate no dichotomy between our "religious" and "secular" lives. I use the term "vocational Christian service" to identify the instances when the ministry is a person's primary source of livelihood.

As people called to walk in a manner worthy of the Lord, we all have the privilege of knowing, loving, and serving Him. Yet we can serve Him in a variety of ways. So this appendix is written as an option to consider—not to twist anyone's arm to go into a full time ministry.

After we have committed ourselves to the Lord and His purposes, and as we experience His love and forgiveness, our next question can be, "In what part of the harvest does God want me to serve?" No roles are holier than others. The Lord is far more concerned with our hearts than with our vocations, but our jobs are significant nonetheless.

Some people have the misconception that those who go into the ministry are committed to Christ, but those who go into a secular job aren't. Bosh! A person's vocation is not a thermometer of his spiritual temperature. A person in a secular vocation can be just as committed to Christ as a person in vocational Christian service—maybe more! Whatever vocation we choose is a matter of calling, not commitment.

Our first priority

We should pursue the vocation that we believe God wants us to pursue. One person's call to go into the ministry is no more noble than another's call to become a banker. Both respond to God's will for God's glory in God's harvest field.

But the pressures to live for Christ in a secular environment are enormous. In fact, it is usually more difficult to be a laborer for Christ in a secular job than it is in Christian work. Some people wisely suggest that a Christian going into a secular vocation needs to be even more sure of God's calling than one serving the Lord in vocational Christian service.

When I was a senior at the University of Georgia, I planned to go to law school. I took the law boards in December, anticipating the results in March. But as I waited for the scores, God led me in a different direction.

My friend Tom had been taking me to Christian meetings, showing me how to study the Bible, and praying with me for a couple of months. I was beginning to see that God could use somebody like Tom in an incredible way. People were becoming Christians. Lives were being changed. Maybe, just maybe, He could use me, too.

While attending a conference in Atlanta early that February, several of us were riding around, looking for a restaurant. Our conversation was not about hamburgers; it was about Christian service. A couple of people were extolling the virtues of vocational Christian service. Then somebody said, "What about you, Pat? What do you think?"

I stated categorically, "I'm not going into the ministry."

Bonnie asked, "You aren't willing?"

I retorted, "No way!"

After a little silence, Bonnie softly asked, "Pat, are you willing to be willing?"

After more silence I answered, "Well, uh, yes, I guess so. If God will make me willing, then I guess I would do it."

That was only a tiny crack in the door, but it was a start. At the conference, I started analyzing my reasons for becoming a lawyer. They were obvious: I wanted the money, prestige, and comfort that a law career could provide. I began to realize that someday I'll stand before Christ to give an account of my life. When He asks, "What did you do with the resources I gave you?" I didn't want to have to say, "I spent it on prestige, money, cars, houses, and travel."

I realized that there are a lot of lawyers. If I didn't become one, somebody else would take my place. On the other hand, there is a tremendous shortage of missionaries, and the line of applicants is very short! I heard no voices, saw no visions, experienced no flashing lights. Rather, logic compelled me to make a different decision about what to pursue as my life's vocation.

A few weeks later I got a letter from the University of Georgia law school that contained my board scores and my acceptance to law school. I wasn't excited. In fact, I had almost forgotten about it.

When I told my parents and friends that I had been accepted to law school but I wasn't going, some understood. Others were not pleased at all. They thought I had given up the chance of a lifetime. But it was important for me to be obedient to God.

That was more than fifteen years ago. Since then I have experienced many wonderful times and a few very painful periods, but today I am more committed to serving Christ than ever before.

Don't get me wrong. I am certainly not inferring that the Lord wants everybody to forsake law to go into ministry full-time. But it was His calling for me. It is up to each person to discern the God's direction and will.

A friend of mine with a sincere love for Christ and a servant's heart felt condemned by other Christians when he went into banking. He sensed that the attitude of the people who discipled him was that he should go into full-time Christian work or else! When he didn't, their attitude toward him was not at all sympathetic or understanding.

We need to point people to Christ and motivate them to serve Him wherever they go and whatever they do. With that kind of motivation, some will choose the ministry for a vocation. Those who don't will move into a secular career feeling supported and encouraged instead of defeated and condemned.

No good excuses

A legitimate reason to avoid vocational Christian service is if God specifically calls you into the secular job market as your field of Christian service and where you can provide for your family. But there are also many excuses that aren't valid.

One of the big excuses is: "Now that I have my degree, I owe it to Christ to succeed so others will respect and listen to me." The statement sounds good, but it is often riddled with deception. It expressess a thinly veiled pursuit of success and recognition, justified by the idea that those things will earn a platform for ministry. Our responsibility to Christ is to obey, not to succeed. If success comes as we obey, we can indeed use it as a platform for ministry. But our primary focus must be obedience, not success.

Some people say they can't go into vocational Christian service because they are stewards of the time, effort, and money they've invested getting a degree in engineering, law, business, or nursing. But effective stewardship requires setting priorities. For example, I spent time, money, and effort learning to play tennis. In college, I played about five times a week. It was an important part of my life. But when my children were born, I realized that they were far more important than my tennis game. So during the past six years, I've averaged playing only three or four times a year.

Am I a bad steward of the time and money I've devoted to practice, rackets, and balls? No. I've chosen a higher calling. The same principle holds true on a larger scale. Just because you do something well or have a degree doesn't necessarily mean that you are obligated to continue in that field. Otherwise, Jesus would have stayed in carpentry, Paul would have remained a scholarly tent maker, and Peter would have kept fishing. The stewardship of God's grace involves a higher calling than skills, education, or vocational experience. The question remains: "What does God want you to do?"

Financial instability is another excuse to avoid full-time ministry. Some say, "I can't go into the ministry. I'm in debt up to my ears!" This is often true.

If you are young, beware of accumulating financial obligations that will lock you into the necessity of working long hours to keep creditors off your back. If you are already in debt, work yourself out through prudent savings and frugal spending so you can "owe nothing to anyone except to love one another" (Romans 13:8). Only then will you be available to do whatever God wants you to do in the business community or in vocational Christian service.

Parental disapproval is another reason (perhaps the main one) why some people don't consider a vocational Christian ministry. At one time Christian ministry was a dream many parents had for their children's lives. Not so today. Now you are more likely to hear students say, "My parents would kill me if I went into the ministry!"

Some parents ask their children, "Will you starve?" "Are you going to embarrass me?" "Will your eyes glaze over?" Such parents have a deep suspicion about the ministry. This suspicion is a barrier for those who desire parental approval.

Desires for comfort, prestige, and riches keep others from even considering the ministry as a vocation. They don't want to limit income possibilities. Rich tastes, prestige, and travel overpower appreciation for Christ. Who wants to suffer?

I've heard some people say, "I'm not called to the ministry, so I'm going into business (or nursing, law, or whatever)." What some of these people mean is: "God didn't bludgeon me over the head and make me become a missionary, so I'm going to make money, have a nice home and car, and travel. I'll join a church where I can be spiritually fed, and I'll help out a little." This attitude does not reflect a desire to love and serve Christ.

None of these reasons are new. But they are tragically effective in stopping people from doing what God wants them to do.

Reevaluating

The leader of a Christian organization at Texas A & M told me that many freshmen and sophomore students express a

desire to go into a vocational Christian service. But by the time
they become juniors or seniors, the reality of parental disapproval and the lure of worldly prestige and comfort have taken
their toll. Even though the students had great dreams of serving
Christ in their first two years of college, those dreams are too
often replaced by a growing commitment to careers in business
or professional fields. Strong leadership and clear teaching on
biblical values are needed so we don't allow the deceitfulness of
the world to choke out the truth of God's Word and make us
unfruitful (Matthew 13:22).

Those who see the deception and emptiness of selfish
ambition will choose Jesus over such empty promises. These
people see serving Christ as the only logical option in life.
They disregard what others think to gladly serve Him and bear
fruit for the kingdom (Matthew 13:23).

The calling of God is first to His Lordship. Then He calls
us to be laborers in His harvest field. And finally, He directs us
to the portion of the field that He chooses for us. Some will be
directed to serve Him through evangelism and discipleship,
others as barbers, lawyers, salesmen, nurses or whatever. Where
is He calling you?

QUESTIONS

1. *What are the reasons you chose (are choosing) your
   vocational path?*

2. *For the sake of reflection, assume that God is leading
   you into vocational Christian service. What would be
   the major barriers for you?*

3. *If you stood before Christ today, and He asked,
   "What did you do with the resources I entrusted to
   you?" what would you tell Him?*

4. How would considering vocational Christian service
    affect your:

    relationship with Christ—

    priorities—

    relationships with others—

    ministry—

5. Read Matthew 9:35-38. Why did Jesus see the needs
    of people so clearly? After He instructed the disciples
    to pray, what did He tell them to do? (See Matthew
    10:1-5.) Where is the best place for you to serve
    Christ? Why?

Appendix B:
Further Study From the Bible

Matthew	Mark	Luke	John	Purpose
5:10-16	1:29-39	6:20-38	5:44	Matt. 22:36-39
5:29, 30/18:7-9	3:31-35	6:39-49	6:26-40	Matt. 13:44-46
6:1-24	4:1-20	7:36-50	6:41-71	Phil. 3:7-10
6:25-34/7:7-11	4:21-34	8:4-18	7:7-17	Psalm 27:4
7:13-27	7:1-23	9:18-26	7:37-39	Psalm 73:25-28
9:35-38	8:14-21	9:57-62	8:12	John 17:3
10:24-33	8:27-38	10:1-24	8:31-47	Jer. 9:23, 24
10:34-42	9:33-41	10:25-37	10:1-30	
11:2-6	9:42-50	10:38-42	10:31-39	
11:28-30	10:13-16	11:21-26	11:25, 26	
12:34-37	10:17-31	12:1-12	12:1-8	
13:1-23	10:35-45	12:13-34	12:20-36	
13:44-46	11:20-26	12:49-53	12:44-50	
16:24-27	12:28-34	13:22-30	13:1-20	

Matthew	Mark	Luke	John
18:21-35	12:38-40	14:7-11	13:34, 35
19:16-26	12:41-44	14:12-24	14:1-31
19:27-30	14:1-11	14:25-35	15:1-27
20:20-38	16:14-18	16:15	16:1-33
22:35-40		16:19-31	17:1-26
23:1-15		17:7-10	21:15-23
24:32--25:30		18:9-14	
25:31-46		18:15-30	
26:1-13		19:11-27	
28:18-20		21:10-19	
		22:24-27	
		24:46-49	

The above passages describe why it is reasonable to live in abject, reckless abandonment to Christ. Study one or two a day, asking (and writing down your responses to) the following questions according to II Timothy 3:16, 17:

1. *What does this passage teach you? (Observation and interpretation)*

2. *Do you fall short? In what way? (Reproof)*

3. *What changes do you need to make? (Correction)*

4. *How can you incorporate these changes into your weekly schedule? (Training in righteousness)*